THE CROSSING OF THE WAYS

THE CROSSING OF THE WAYS

William Faulkner, the South, and the Modern World

KARL F. ZENDER

Library of Congress Cataloging-in-Publication Data

Zender, Karl F., 1937–
The crossing of the ways : William Faulkner, the South, and the modern world / Karl F. Zender.
p. cm.
Bibliography: p.
Includes index
ISBN 0-8135-1349-9 ISBN 0-8135-1376-6 (pbk.)
1. Faulkner, William, 1897–1962—Criticism and interpretation.
2. Southern States in literature. I. Title.
PS3511.A86Z9875 1989
813′.52—dc19 88-15872
CIP

British Cataloging-in-Publication information available

Manufactured in the United States of America

To the memory of my father
Franz Josef Zender
and of my mother
Rose Grimes Zender

Contents

Preface

This book is a study of the evolution of William Faulkner's art, as revealed through his use and reuse of selected themes and motifs. Organized thematically and chronologically, it focuses on the mature fiction, particularly on the novels written after 1935. Each chapter takes up a separate theme or motif—sound, money and materiality, freedom and responsibility, imagination, education—and examines its use in a single novel or a related group of novels. With the exception of Chapter One, which provides an overview of Faulkner's career and which establishes a frame of reference for the rest of the book, the primary discussions of the novels occur in chronological order, beginning with *Pylon* and *The Wild Palms* in Chapter Two and ending with *The Mansion* in the Epilogue.

Three purposes govern this study. In a well-known 1935 essay entitled "The Profession of Letters in the South," Allen Tate discusses the relation between "the considerable achievement of Southerners in modern American letters" and the "peculiarly historical consciousness of the Southern writer" (533). This relation, he says, "is quite temporary"; it is "a crossing of the ways, not unlike, on an infinitesimal scale, the outburst of poetic genius at the end of the sixteenth century when commercial England had already begun to crush feudal England" (533). Tate's comment expresses a view of the situation of the southern artist widely held during the years when Faulkner was active as a writer. I believe that Faulkner himself held this view and that he understood his own artistic situation in essentially the terms it provides. My first purpose, therefore, and my main one, is to analyze the effect on Faulkner's art of the disappearance of a traditional South and of the emergence of a modern, deregionalized America. My interest in this topic is literary and aesthetic, not sociological or historical. The social, economic, and cultural changes occurring in the South during Faulkner's lifetime were far-reaching and profound, but they will appear in these pages only to the extent that they are represented directly in Faulkner's fiction. Rather, I will examine how Faulkner uses the disappearance of the pre-modern South expressively, as a way of exploring the relation of his artistic identity to experiences of loss and of defining (and redefining) his subject matter.

My second purpose is to add to our understanding of Faulkner's creative process, particularly of its conscious, intellectual aspects. In a popular guide to twentieth-century literature, published in 1976, Martin Seymour-Smith groups Faulkner with "the great non-intellectual novelists of the century," saying that Faulkner "worked essentially from intuition and passion and never from what an educated man would call thought" (115). Much has been done in recent years to counter this reductive view of our greatest writer as a modern version of Milton's Shakespeare, warbling his native woodnotes wild. One thinks, for example, of the emerging new-literary-historical reading of Faulkner's fiction as a meditation on the material and ideological bases of modern culture; one thinks also of the continuing elucidation, by both old- and new-style intellectual historians, of Faulkner's indebtedness to a romantic tradition of thought about the nature of artistic representation. This book contributes to both these efforts. In Chapter One I use contrasting ideas of sound—as a trope for poetic inspiration and as a medium of popular culture—to explore Faulkner's quarrel with modernity. In Chapters Two and Three, I examine the relation between Faulkner's narcissistic and privative understanding of his artistic identity and his sense of himself as a wage earner, property owner, and commercial artist. In Chapters Four and Five, I explore the problems surrounding Faulkner's attempts to subordinate his essentially subversive understanding of the function of art to ethically and socially ameliorative ends. Throughout the book, I seek to demonstrate the adaptivity of Faulkner's thought, how by a continuous process of refinement and redefinition he adjusts his artistic self-understanding to alterations in his personal, cultural, and literary circumstances.

My third purpose reveals itself in the greater-than-usual emphasis I give to the post-World War II fiction; it is to provide a fresh approach to the novels of this period. My emphasis on the late fiction came about somewhat against my will, for, like most readers, I am convinced that the great phase of Faulkner's career extends from *The Sound and the Fury* to *Go Down, Moses,* and it is the fiction of this period that I prefer to discuss. But as I worked my way into this project, I found myself returning again and again to my vexed sense that we have not yet learned how to read the postwar novels adequately. By and large, readers of the late novels have been caught between the Scylla of blanket dismissal and the Charybdis of searching for virtues similar in kind to those found in the novels of the great middle period. The innovation I bring to the reading of the late novels is modest but, I hope, useful. It consists of shifting the issue of judgment and evaluation from the reader to Faulkner himself. Throughout this book, I treat the creative decline of the postwar years as a fact of Faulkner's own experience, and I explore how he converts this fact into a fictional theme. Approaching the late novels in this way allows me to read them reflexively, as works in which Faulkner, like Yeats, Wordsworth, and others before him, transforms the threatened departure of his creative power into a source of its renewal. It also allows me to discuss the not inconsiderable merits of these novels without making insupportable claims of equivalence with the earlier fiction.

Acknowledgments

Early versions of the first four chapters of this book appeared in *PMLA* (99 [1984]: 89–108), *The Faulkner Journal* (1, no. 2 [1986]: 17–29), *The Southern Review* (n.s. 17 [1981]: 288–302) and *Faulkner and Race: Proceedings of the Thirteenth Annual Faulkner and Yoknapatawpha Conference* (Jackson: University Press of Mississippi, 1988, 272–296). I am grateful to the editors of these journals and conference proceedings for permission to reprint this material. I am also grateful to Jill Faulkner Summers, executrix of the William Faulkner Estate, for permission to quote from letters in the William Faulkner Collections, Manuscripts Department, University of Virginia Library.

At several stages in its development, the manuscript of this book was the beneficiary of helpful readings. I wish to thank Max Byrd, Joanne Feit Diehl, Sandra Gilbert, Anne Jones, David Minter, Stephen Ross, and David Wyatt for their stimulating comments and suggestions for improvement. Three people deserve special thanks for their extraordinary service on behalf of this project. For years, Jeffrey Duncan has provided insightful readings of my work and has allowed me to take sustenance from his optimism. The chair of my department, Michael Hoffman, not only read and commented on several sections of the manuscript but also provided released time from teaching at a stage crucial to the completion of the project. Dean Dickerson of Davis, California, has for some time supported my scholarly and critical endeavors in ways too various to name. Most of all (always most of all) I wish to thank my wife, Lynn Zender, who never allowed her healthy skepticism about literary study to interfere with her ability to listen, to commiserate, and to give me hope.

My mind turns now, as it does so often, to the two people to whom this book is dedicated. My father came to this country from Germany in 1927; my mother grew up in the hills of southern Ohio. Neither went past the eighth grade in school. They did not read Faulkner, but they appreciated such beauty as their circumstances afforded them, and they loved wit and the play of ideas. I will always be in their debt.

THE CROSSING OF THE WAYS

The soul and body rive not more in parting
Than greatness going off.

William Shakespeare
Antony and Cleopatra

ONE

The Power of Sound

Near the end of his account of Addie Bundren's funeral in *As I Lay Dying,* Vernon Tull describes the impression made on him by the women's singing:

> In the thick air it's like their voices come out of the air, flowing together and on in the sad, comforting tunes. When they cease it's like they hadn't gone away. It's like they had just disappeared into the air and when we moved we would loose them again out of the air around us, sad and comforting (86).

To the seasoned reader of Faulkner's fiction, Tull's comment will seem familiar, resembling as it does so many of Faulkner's other descriptions of sound. For Tull, as sooner or later for most of Faulkner's major characters, sound is a mysterious, almost tangible force. It appears to be ubiquitous and sourceless, even when its source is known. It is animate, and it seems to reside in the air, either in the form of voices, as here and in *The Sound and the Fury* and *Absalom, Absalom!,* or in the form of the "vast, abateless hum" of physical nature (*Intruder in the Dust* 129). It can offer comfort, as it does to Tull, but it can also threaten to overwhelm the hearer or to consume the speaker, as it does in *The Sound and the Fury, Requiem for a Nun,* and several other novels.[1]

Such a frequently used and variously elaborated motif can bear many meanings. One in particular is central to this chapter. To speak of "voices" that "come out of the air" inevitably evokes ideas of the muse and of poetic inspiration. Tull, of course, is too matter-of-fact to express such ideas directly, but other Faulkner characters—most notably his *artistes manqués* like Quentin Compson and Darl Bundren—are not so limited. As we watch such characters struggle to understand and to control the voices that surround them, we sense that we are in the presence of a sustained meditation on the artist's power. Faulkner came to this meditation early and stayed with it long, and he consistently used images of sound as a main vehicle for its expression. As his career advanced, the terms of the meditation, the personal significance that it held for him, and the images that he used to express it all underwent radical change. Examining Faulkner's uses of sound, then, should afford us insight into the evolution of his understanding of himself as an artist.

I

The idea of a voice that descends from the air is, of course, one that Faulkner could have inherited from almost any writer in the Western tradition from Homer and Hesiod on down; but romantic and postromantic uses of the idea appear to have influenced him most. We therefore should begin by considering for a moment the recent history of the muse. As Meyer Abrams demonstrates, a central effect of the romantic revolution in belief was "to naturalize the supernatural and to humanize the divine" (*Natural Supernaturalism* 68). The muse was not exempt from this process. When the romantic poets relocated heaven and hell inside the human mind, they did so because they had lost the ability to believe that these ideas denoted literal attributes of the physical world. The historical change to which they were responding is a familiar one: as the closed term of earlier conceptions of the past gave way to geological time, so the three-story universe of heaven above, hell below, and earth between gave way to Copernican astronomy and Newtonian physics. Hesiod's muses descend from above, as does Milton's Urania; but already for Milton, the three-story universe had become an ambiguous concept, never completely affirmed or denied. And when Wordsworth in his turn calls on "Urania . . . or a greater muse" to "descend" from "highest heaven" and help him relocate Milton's epic theme inside the human mind, he makes only figurative use of the motif of the descent of the goddess (*The Recluse* 200). For him, as for almost all later writers, the old language of a physical descent is unrelated to the world of experience. The muse cannot come down from heaven, because heaven, wherever else it may be, is not above us.

Viewed in this broad perspective, Faulkner's voices that come out of the air can be seen to extend a central tendency of romantic thought. Like his predecessors, Faulkner was engaged in naturalizing a concept that in earlier history had been understood in supernatural terms. But for him, as for many other heirs of the romantic tradition, this process of naturalization had ambiguous implications. The image of the muse as an external visitant has the capacity to symbolize not only the supernatural but also the cultural dependence of the artist. Initially, then—for someone like Shelley, for example—desacralizing the muse must have resulted in a sense of increased freedom and power. By depriving the muse of her objective status, the romantic poets were expressing their Promethean aspiration to be the sole source of their own inspiration—to be, that is, autonomous artists. But accompanying this revolutionary quest for autonomy was a reciprocal and perhaps inevitable movement into isolation and alienation. As the muse lost her objective status, poets came to relocate her in their own minds, where she served to symbolize their inward and idiosyncratic visionary power. They were only able to appropriate the muse for this purpose because the culture at large was willing to give her up. During the course of the nineteenth and early twentieth centuries, the naturalizing process that began as a translation of sacred ideas into their secular equivalents gradually produced a general cultural denial of the value of visionary experience. As this happened, artists—specifically those of Faulkner's era—found themselves cut off from their own culture. Caught between their sense of the authenticity of their visionary power and the skepticism or indifference of the culture at large, they were forced into either psychic or actual exile.[2]

These overall considerations can help to explain Faulkner's deeply equivocal depictions of sound. Many of his images of sound suggest a yearning for reconciliation. By displacing voice from his fictional characters outward into the physical scene, Faulkner suggests that the tension between artist and culture—or, more broadly, between self and other, subject and object, mind and nature—can be resolved. Time and again in his fiction, the world murmurs, hums, and whispers with a more than natural voice. Humanized, it suggests the possibility that it is congruent with the hearer and responsive to his or her needs. Yet more frequently than not, Faulkner surrounds his images of reconciliation with ironic qualifications. Also, as time passes his depictions of sound undergo a fundamental alteration. With increasing frequency as his career progresses, Faulkner uses images of sound to express, not reciprocity between the self and the other, but rather an invasion of the self *by* the other. The voices that reside in the air—or, alternatively, in the minds of his characters—begin less to resemble the muse than some dark opposite, and in their ability to overwhelm the characters who unwillingly listen to them, they suggest that a tragic incongruity lies at the heart of the individual's relation with the world.

Faulkner discovered the broad outlines of how he wished to use images of sound quite early in his career. Almost from the beginning, what might be called positive images of sound—that is, images of reconciliation—can readily be found in his writings. Although these images take a variety of forms, they usually depict an individual in a space defined by sound. The space is often physically bounded as well—it can be a garden, a valley, a church, a cave—but whether it is bounded or not, a reciprocal relation whose medium of expression is sound always exists between the individual and the surrounding scene. In *The Marionettes,* for example, the play that Faulkner wrote in 1920, the congruence between Marietta and the garden in which she innocently resides is signified by the song of her nightingales, which is "woven about" the garden "like cloth of gold" (31). In "Nympholepsy," an early prose sketch, the nameless protagonist stands at twilight before a "green cathedral of trees," entranced by the sound of "the day repeating slow orisons in a green nave" (405). And in *The Marble Faun,* Faulkner's ambitious early poem cycle, a wide variety of images of sound express the faun's longing for release from his "marble bonds" (12) and for entry into a living union with the world.

From early in his career, then, Faulkner created images in which sound functions as an agency of reconciliation between the self and the other. From the outset too, he developed ironic checks and controls that suggest the ephemerality of the wished-for reconciliation. In *The Marionettes,* for example, the garden enclosed by the nightingales' song is invaded by sound of a different sort when Pierrot sings his song of seduction to Marietta. When she first responds to his song, she discovers that "the nightingales that once sung in my garden have flown" (11); and when she returns from her night of amorous adventure, no longer a virgin, she finds that the nightingales' music has been replaced by the "cacophonous cries of . . . peacocks" (51). Similarly, in *The Marble Faun,* the return of the faun to his state of frozen isolation is signaled by "a blatant crowd" of dancers, who invade the garden to the accompaniment of "brass horns horrible and loud" (46). Finally, to cite a somewhat later example, we may note the importance of sound in the scene outside the Negro church at the end of *Soldiers' Pay.* Faulkner explicitly says that the singing coming from the church expresses "all the longing of mankind for a Oneness with Something, somewhere" (319). But in this scene, as in the one it foreshadows in the fourth section of *The Sound and the Fury,* Faulkner denies the main characters of the novel the emotional reconciliation that the church service symbolizes. Joe Gilligan and the Reverend Mahon can listen to the singing; but because they cannot participate in it, they must finally walk away, "feeling dust in their shoes" (319).

When we turn to the images of sound in the mature fiction, we find that they express a similar desire for reconciliation and a similar ironic doubt about the possibility of achieving it. Along with this continuity come significant changes in artistic method and in emphasis. As David Minter writes in *William Faulkner: His Life and Work,* in his early poetry Faulkner deprived himself of almost every subject matter except "his own more obvious emotions and the words of other poets" (73). Because Faulkner believed that poetry has "no room at all for trash" but instead had to be "absolutely impeccable, absolutely perfect" (*Faulkner in the University* 207), he tended to locate both his poetry and his early, poemlike prose sketches in a mythical, abstract world as uncontaminated as possible by the particularities of the world in which he actually lived. Although he began to break with this abstracting and universalizing tendency as early as *Soldiers' Pay,* not until he wrote *Flags in the Dust* did he fully direct his art toward what he later called his "own little postage stamp of native soil" (*Lion in the Garden* 255). Once he did so, his images of sound, like the whole range of his other imagery, gained enormously in evocative power. In contrast to the attenuated imagery of the early prose and poetry, the aural images of Faulkner's great fiction have their origin in the concrete and highly distinctive voices and sounds of his own region. In instances as various as the "Chuck. Chuck. Chuck" of the adze in *As I Lay Dying* (5), the call of the Carolina wren at the beginning of *Sanctuary,* and the "sharp and brittle crack and clatter" of Armstid's wagon as it approaches the waiting Lena Grove in *Light in August* (5), we see Faulkner using images of sound to evoke the life of his region in all its density and particularity.

The dominant impression created by these and similar images is of a valued world recaptured. As Faulkner himself said in an unpublished note written around 1931, *Flags in the Dust*—and, by implication, the other Yoknapatawpha novels as well—originated in a desire "to bind into a whole [a] world which for some reason I believe should not pass utterly out of the memory of man."[3] In his loving evocation of the voices, sounds, and other sensations of his native region, Faulkner provides us with a way of entering into reconciling union with a world from which, however indirectly, most of us feel ourselves to have sprung. Yet we should not permit the powerful sense of *le temps retrouvé* that we so often experience in Faulkner's mature fiction to obscure our awareness of his increasing tendency to ascribe inimical qualities to sound. What happens in the great fiction of the late 1920s and 1930s is not merely a parallel growth in the evocative power of images of reconciliation and images of alienation but a substantial shift in emphasis as well. Where in his early poetry and prose Faulkner's attention had been more or less evenly divided between positive and negative images, in the middle phase of his career he begins to tip the balance in favor of images of sound as an invasive force.

There are several reasons for this increased emphasis on the inimical power of sound. In part it occurs because Faulkner's acceptance of his native region as a worthy subject for his art produced a heightened awareness of the destructive power of time. Implicit in his effort at preserving the vanishing world of his youth is a sense of the evanescence of reconciliation. In his early prose and poetry, Faulkner emphasizes cyclical conceptions of time, with the consequence that he presents both reconciliation and alienation as recurrent conditions: in *The Marble Faun,* for example, Pan's music symbolizes the renewal of life that comes with the onset of spring; hence the faun's joy over his own, and the world's, renewal can be expected to recur with equal intensity in each coming year. But when Faulkner directs his art toward the changing life of his own region, his characters' experiences of wholeness become fleeting, merely momentary, chance evasions of their awareness of time's flight. Again and again in his mature fiction, Faulkner allows his characters to pause for a moment, enraptured by harmonious sound—"a steady golden sound, as of sunlight become audible" (*Flags in the Dust* 56)—only to have some hostile form of sound intrude and return them to the world of time and loss.

A second reason for Faulkner's increasing ascription of inimical qualities to sound is a change in his attitude toward his native region that began with the writing of *The Sound and the Fury*. The relatively straightforward nostalgia for a vanishing world that had led to the writing of *Flags in the Dust* was transformed into the much more complex attitude that Faulkner later described as "loving [his native land] even while hating some of it" (*Essays* 36). As Faulkner suggests in an unpublished introduction to *The Sound and the Fury* written in 1933, this shift in attitude led to a deeper understanding of his artistic purpose, for it allowed him to combine his desire "to escape . . . into a makebelieve region of swords and magnolias and mockingbirds" with his desire "to draw a savage indictment of the contemporary scene."[4] When this more complex purpose comes into play in Faulkner's fiction, images and forms of sound that had formerly been presented as benign become equivocal or even entirely hostile. Thus, to cite only two examples among many, the "mellow snatches of [Negro] laughter" (154) that serve as a sentimental and largely unexamined backdrop to the action of *Flags in the Dust* take on a problematic quality when they recur in *Absalom, Absalom!* as the "roaring waves of mellow laughter meaningless and terrifying and loud" (232) that haunt the young Thomas Sutpen; and the tales and sounds of the Civil War that Virginia Du Pre uses to evoke the Sartoris family's heroic past in *Flags in the Dust* undergo a similar transformation when they pass into Gail Hightower's life-evading fantasy of "the wild bugles and the clashing sabres and the dying thunder of hooves" in *Light in August* (467).

A third and somewhat more involved reason for Faulkner's growing interest in the hostile power of sound is a change that occurred in his understanding of the power and limits of the imagination. Like most other heirs of the romantic tradition, Faulkner believed that the imagination shapes our knowledge of the world. In the early part of his career, he toyed with an extreme, solipsistic form of this belief in which he ascribed to the imagination a capacity not only to shape our perceptions but to alter external reality itself; and he associated this notion with images of sound as a transforming force projected forth by the mind into the world. Making his native region the subject of his art helped to abate this dream of imaginative omnipotence, for the world that he then began to depict was too rich and varied to be thought of merely as the passive recipient of the transforming power of the imagination. Hence Faulkner, while not abandoning his belief in the imagination's ability to shape perception, began to acknowledge the independence of the world, which he now envisioned as possessing equal reality with the mind.[5]

As Faulkner himself recognized, this change in his understanding of the relation between the mind and the world released him for his earlier artistic self-absorption. In the "shadowy but ingenious shapes" that he had begun to create, as he says in his note on *Flags in the Dust,* he found a way in which he "might reaffirm the impulses of [his] own ego in this actual world" (Blotner, "William Faulkner's Essay" 124). Yet abandoning his dream of imaginative omnipotence also produced a heightened sense of the world's dangerous otherness and of the hostile power of sound. If the imagination could not control external reality, then alien aspects of the world—alien sounds—could at their own discretion enter and overwhelm the mind. Hence in Faulkner's mature fiction the sounds of the mind and the sounds of the world reverse polarity, with the sounds of the mind losing projective power and the sounds of the world gaining it. The sounds of the mind begin increasingly to display a defensive quality, as Faulkner's characters seek to create a protective barrier—a "screen of words" (*Flags in the Dust* 272)—between themselves and the sounds, now grown bold, mobile, and intrusive, of the external world.

II

The character who most fully embodies the complex attitudes toward sound characteristic of Faulkner's great middle phase is Quentin Compson in *The Sound and the Fury*. Beneath his yearning for death lies a nostalgia for home as strong as any found in Faulkner's fiction. Here as elsewhere, a main vehicle for the expression of this nostalgia is sound: the "laboring sound of the exhaust and groaning wheels" (100) of the train that carries Quentin home for Christmas, the sound of the school bell that released him to freedom when he was a child, and, most memorably, the sound of Louis Hatcher calling in his dogs at the end of an evening of hunting. Quentin's evocation of this last sound is perhaps the most remarkable example of reconciling sound to be found anywhere in Faulkner's fiction. The occasion is an invidious comparison that Quentin draws between New England and the South. New England, he says, is a desiccated land, "brooding and nursing every niggard stone," whereas the South as he remembers it possesses "a kind of still and violent fecundity that satisfie[s] even bread-hunger like" (129).

This vision of the South as a source of sustenance receives elaboration when Quentin turns to the images of sound at the heart of the passage. The air in New England, he says, is so old that "even sound seemed to fail in [it], like the air was worn out with carrying sounds so long"; but the air in the South, "flowing around you," is so full of sustaining sounds as to seem almost like a living being (129–130). While listening to the dogs, Quentin says, "we'd sit in the dry leaves that whispered a little with the slow respiration of our waiting and with the slow breathing of the earth and the windless October" (131); and when Louis Hatcher would finally call in the dogs, his voice, far from severing Quentin's connection to this living world, became a further form of attachment to it. "He sounded," Quentin says, "just like the horn he carried slung on his shoulder and never used, but clearer, mellower, as though his voice were a part of darkness and silence, coiling out of it, coiling into it again. WhoOoooo. WhoOoooo. WhoOoooooooooooooooo" (132). Here, as in Vernon Tull's description of the singing at Addie's funeral, voice and air, desire and the world, are integrated so plangently, so completely, and so movingly as to reduce us to silent approbation and to wonder.[6]

Yet poised against this memory of reconciling sound are a host of memories in which sound functions as a hostile and intrusive force. Throughout the second section of the novel, Faulkner places into conflict with Quentin's dream of reconciliation his own growing awareness of the evanescence of all forms of union with the world. Infusing this conflict, and ensuring the eventual defeat of Quentin's dream, is an agonized sense of what Lewis P. Simpson calls the "entire inherence of body and spirit in the historical process" ("Faulkner and the Legend of the Artist" 97). In this phrase, Simpson refers to the modern tendency—of which the desacralizing of the muse can serve as an example—to interpret in historical and cultural terms matters that formerly had been thought to be entirely natural or supernatural. This mode of interpretation is of course fundamental to our modern understanding of existence: under its aegis, the most intimate and the most far-reaching aspects of our relation with the world—our sexuality, family ties, memory and sense of time, even our consciousness itself—have revealed their "inherence" in history and culture. Yet, as Simpson writes, these revelations have created in the modern individual an "experience of undefinable remorse. . . . [as] an arrangement of human relations that seemed to embody both a natural and mystical permanence" instead reveals itself to be "the embodiment of a process of fundamental alteration" (88).[7]

This sort of remorse is central to Quentin's existence. It stems from his awareness of the relentless ability of history and culture—or, in his terms, of time and family—to appropriate aspects of existence that formerly had seemed to provide refuges for the self. In particular, nature and memory, portrayed as such refuges from the romantic period on, reveal to Quentin their dependent status. Momentarily entranced though he is by his memory of Louis Hatcher's voice and by its promise of union with nature, he cannot finally believe that either memory or nature can truly give him solace. For him they are not autonomous, unchanging dimensions of existence, as they had seemed, but alter in meaning and value over time; and because he finds all forms of change repugnant, he comes to view both of them as hostile forces, intent on invading his consciousness and overwhelming his sense of identity.

Quentin's reactions to sound reveal his sense of the inauthenticity of nature and memory. For him, the sounds of nature—and, of course, its sights and smells as well—have lost their innocence. As he recognizes, once nature is seen to be relative to history and culture, it becomes doubly unsatisfactory as a refuge, for it neither offers the stability of a fixed meaning nor remains subordinate to whatever private meaning an individual might attempt to ascribe to it. He despises the smell of honeysuckle, for example, both because he cannot keep from associating it with the sexual impulses whose presence in himself he wishes to deny and because it suggests to him the disappearance of all stable meaning. "After the honeysuckle got all mixed up in it," he says, ". . . I seemed to be lying neither asleep nor awake looking down a long corridor of grey halflight where all stable things had become shadowy paradoxical all I had done shadows all I had felt suffered taking visible form antic and perverse mocking without relevance inherent themselves with the denial of the significance they should have affirmed" (194–195). In much the same way, he recognizes that both the sounds of nature and associated forms of human sound are neither independent of his culture nor amenable to his control. In his physical distaste for "the rasping of crickets" (172), his sense that he has been trapped in the "smells and sounds of night . . . like under a slack tent" (173), his reluctant awareness of the power of bells to denote the passing of time, and his fear of the "soft girlvoices lingering in the shadowy places" (169), he reveals a thoroughgoing sense that the sounds of his world have been co-opted by the alien meanings of his culture.[8]

Even more than his loss of nature as a refuge, the images of sound in the second section of *The Sound and the Fury* reveal Quentin's loss of faith in the regenerative power of memory. These two forms of loss are of course interconnected, for Quentin's discovery that nature inheres in history and culture necessarily diminishes his ability to make his "memory be as a dwelling-place," to use Wordsworth's phrase, "for all sweet sounds and harmonies" of the physical world ("Tintern Abbey" 100). Along with the withdrawal from his memory of the sustaining sounds of nature, almost all comfort-giving forms of human speech disappear as well. As Stephen M. Ross notes, Quentin's memory is largely composed of voices; in his mind, people are "distinguished by what they say and how they talk, not by what they do or how they look" ("Loud World" 252). Almost all these remembered voices are painful to him. Only Louis Hatcher persists as a strongly positive vocal memory; as for the rest of the voices from Quentin's past, the forms they take indicate the burden of pain and disappointment they carry: in Quentin's memory, Benjy is the sound of his bellowing, hammering "*back and forth between the walls in waves*" (143), Mrs. Compson is "*a voice weeping steadily and softly beyond [a] twilit door*" (108), and Mr. Compson is the remote, cynically disengaged "Father said" whose counsel of despair pervades Quentin's mind on the last day of his life.[9]

For Quentin, the voices of his memory are the internal symbols of his alienation, as the smells and sounds of nature are the external ones. In his unequal struggle with these voices, smells, and sounds, we see his inability to defend himself against the invasive power of his culture. About all he can do in self-defense is put his own voice into contention with the voices and sounds that threaten him, by making it an instrument with which either to escape or to attack the world. Thus he confesses, or imagines he confesses, to having committed incest with Caddy because he hopes by speaking his desire "to isolate her out of the loud world" and to make "the sound of it . . . be as though it had never been" (203); he tries to make Caddy speak of her sexual experiences for much the same reason, as she guesses when she asks "*do you think that if I say it it wont be*" (140); and he repeatedly imagines, in an image of projected sound reminiscent of Faulkner's early works, that "*Quentin has shot Herbert he shot his voice through the floor of Caddy's room*" (120–121; cf. Ross, "Loud World").

Unlike Faulkner's earlier writings, however, the second section of *The Sound and the Fury* subjects the dream of a transforming power of voice to ironic scrutiny. Faulkner undermines Quentin's dream of verbal omnipotence in a variety of ways: by subjecting it to Caddy and Mr. Compson's skeptical commentary, by contrasting it with the ineffectuality of Quentin's actual verbal encounters with Herbert Head and Dalton Ames, and—most tellingly—by restricting the arena of its expression to Quentin's mind. In a question-and-answer session at the University of Virginia, Faulkner was asked whether Quentin actually had said to his father that he had committed incest with Caddy. Faulkner replied, "He never did. He said, If I were brave, I would—I might say this to my father, whether it was a lie or not, or if I were—if I would say this to my father, maybe he would answer me back the magic word which would relieve me of this anguish and agony I live with. No, they were imaginary" (*Faulkner in the University* 262). In emphasizing so strongly the purely imaginary status of Quentin's quest for a "magic word," Faulkner confirms the impression created in most readers by the novel itself. When Mr. Compson asks, "did you try to make her do it," Quentin answers "i was afraid to i was afraid she might and then it wouldnt have done any good but if i could tell you we did it would have been so" (203). In offering this response, Quentin reveals that his dream of omnipotence masks an underlying despair about the possibility of ever truly affecting the world. By rejecting the movement from word to deed and instead confining his statement to a hypothetical—and, in Faulkner's view, imaginary—appeal to his father, Quentin chooses to preserve his dream of omnipotence by refusing to test it. He will keep the dream safe by confining it to his own mind, where he can be both the source and the sole recipient of the transforming power of voice.

Yet even this attempt to establish a fully self-absorbed relation with his own voice does not protect Quentin from the intrusive power of alien sound. As several commentators have noted, Quentin's speech is largely made up of the catch phrases of schoolboy philosophy, turn-of-the-century melodrama, and the southern code of honor.[10] By assigning Quentin such a highly derivative language, Faulkner calls into question the autonomy of Quentin's own voice and hence its ability to serve as a refuge from the sounds of the world. This Quentin himself reluctantly realizes when he confronts Dalton Ames, for he then hears his voice betray him. In telling Ames "Ill give you until sundown to leave town" (183), he issues an ultimatum whose phrasing wholly derives from the language of melodrama. In his self-repudiating response to this and similar utterances—"my mouth said it I didnt say it at all" (183)—we see adumbrated his understanding that his voice, no less than nature and memory, inheres in the world he seeks to reject. Once he comes to this knowledge, the only way left for him to escape the hostile power of the world's sounds is by doing away entirely with his ability to hear them. But even in imagining his condition after death, Quentin finds that he must levy a further demand on the dream of reconciling sound. "The deep water," he says, will be "like wind, like a roof of wind," beneath which will lie his "murmuring bones" (90). No alien sound but the voice of God saying "Rise" will ever penetrate into this self-absorbed murmuring, and even then, as Quentin says in the grim satisfaction of his unbelief, "only the flat-iron [will] come floating up" (91). In death, at least, he expects to find the quiet refuge that his loud world does not afford him.

III

In an uncharacteristically self-revealing comment made late in his career, Faulkner said, "Ishmael is the witness in *Moby Dick* as I am Quentin in *The Sound and the Fury*" (Blotner, *Faulkner: A Biography* 1522).[11] As the above reading should suggest, Faulkner's representation of himself in the figure of Quentin was an act of disengagement, both from the dream of imaginative omnipotence and, paradoxically, from the fear of engulfment that ensued from relinquishing this dream. In depicting the failure of Quentin's voice to control a world filled with hostile sound, Faulkner affirmed his newly-won faith in the power of his own voice to encompass and order the manifold sounds of the world around him.[12] By its nature, this faith needed to be sustained by an ongoing series of proofs: the only way Faulkner could convince himself of the groundlessness of his fear of engulfment was by continuing to succeed, in novel after novel, in imposing artistic order on the world. Yet even a rapid series of such successes could not fully allay his concern, for as early as his 1933 introduction to *The Sound and the Fury,* we find him expressing anxiety about his future as an artist. The one thing he has learned since writing *The Sound and the Fury,* he says, is that the ecstasy it gave him "will not return" (414). To be sure, "the unreluctance to begin, the cold satisfaction in work well and arduously done, is there" (415). But even these secondary gratifications will only continue to exist "as long as I can do it well"; and already he can envision a time "when not only the ecstasy of writing would be gone, but the unreluctance and the something worth saying too" (415).[13]

When we are engrossed in any one of the extraordinary novels that Faulkner wrote during the great middle period of his career, his fear of an eventual loss of creative power must seem an idle one. But as he himself realized, the problem he faced was not only that his artistic voice might someday diminish in strength but that the world of sounds he needed to organize and control was undergoing radical change. In his note on *Flags in the Dust,* he had spoken of the life of his native region as something he was "already preparing to lose and regret" (Blotner, "William Faulkner's Essay" 122). Opposed to this cherished but vanishing world was a world that he called, in the *Sound and the Fury* introduction, the "New South." The sounds of this new world contrast sharply with those of the world whose passing he mourned, for they are the "O yeah[s]" and the "hard r's" of "the young men who sell the gasoline and the waitresses in the restaurants" and the ringing of the "savage and peremptory bells" that hang "over the intersections of quiet and shaded streets where no one save Northern tourists in Cadillacs and Lincolns ever pass [sic] at a gait faster than a horse trots" (411). As Faulkner's career advanced, the sounds of this new world grew more and more intrusive and demanding, even as the sounds of the vanishing world of his youth grew fainter and fainter. It should not surprise us, then, to find that he gradually came to focus his art on these new sounds and, through them, on the troubling question of whether he was to be their master or their victim.

Faulkner's confrontation with the modern world receives its fullest treatment in his postwar fiction, but the main image with which he elaborates it makes its first appearance in *Pylon,* the novel of his middle period in which he most frequently anticipates the concerns of his later career. The image is of amplified sound. By filling the airport rotunda with "the voice of the [race] announcer reverberant and sonorous" (26), Faulkner created an image that served for the rest of his career as his central metaphor for the dehumanizing and alienating power of modern culture. However hostile the voices that invade and overwhelm Quentin Compson, they nonetheless derive from known and human sources. But the "amplified voice" of the race announcer sounds "as though it were the voice of the steel-and-chromium mausoleum itself" (28). It is the quintessential expression of the invasive power of the modern world because it destroys the last vestige of individual control over hearing. In its presence, not even the sorry means of self-defense that Quentin uses are worth considering, for when sound is amplified, it becomes "apocryphal, sourceless, inhuman, ubiquitous, and beyond weariness or fatigue" (39). It truly becomes a property of the air, and although individuals can walk out of its range for a while, it is always there waiting for them when they return, like "some unavoidable and inexplicable phenomenon of nature" (26).

When Faulkner depicts amplified sound in his later work, he again emphasizes his sense of its inimical qualities. Accompanying this repeated emphasis is a troubled awareness of the rather different response characteristic of the American populace as a whole. To Faulkner's dismay, Americans appear willing to assist in their own mental invasion, for in the eagerness with which they seek out the sound of "radios . . . jukeboxes . . . and . . . bellowing amplifiers on the outside walls . . . of . . . stores," he sees expressed their desire never to "be threatened with one second of silence" (*Intruder in the Dust* 237–238). In both the fiction and the nonfiction of the postwar period, Faulkner repeatedly asks how this condition of mass self-betrayal occurred. He provides a comprehensive answer in the prose sections of *Requiem for a Nun,* in a speech that he delivered to the Delta Council in 1952, and in an essay entitled "On Privacy" that he wrote two years later. In all three works he uses images of sound to create a brief metaphoric history of the decline and fall of American democracy.

The essay, the speech, and the novel all begin their accounts of this decline and fall by using images of sound to express the paradisaical quality of life in early America. In the essay and the speech, America in its early days exhibits a kind of primal social harmony in which "individual men and women" speak "as with one simultaneous voice" and "the whole sky of the western hemisphere" echoes with "one loud American affirmation, one vast Yes" (*Essays* 62, 130). In *Requiem for a Nun,* the attractiveness of early America resides not only in the nation's ability to incorporate individuals into a harmonious union but in its restraint in doing so. As Faulkner envisions matters in the novel, the federal government asks of its citizens only that they give it "respect without servility, allegiance without abasement," and in exchange it allows them to remain "free to withdraw" from union with it "at any moment when the two of them [find] themselves no longer compatible" (12). The image of sound used to symbolize this conception of government understandably differs from the ones found in the essay and the speech. Instead of taking the form of a "thunderous affirmation," the sound of democracy appears here simply as "the thin peremptory voice" (10) of the tin horn with which the government mail rider announces his presence in the southern wilderness.

Once this thin, almost unnoticeable sound enters the wilderness, a process begins that ultimately culminates in a "rocket-roar" of noise beating down on the "battered and indomitable head" of modern man (247). The next few sounds heard in the wilderness are as innocuous as the mail rider's horn, but soon an ominous group appears, men who accompany the western and southern advance of civilization with "mouths . . . full of law and order" and "round with the sound of money" (104). With the appearance of this group, Faulkner's images of sound begin to exemplify the growing power of the nation as a whole to destroy the individuality of its members. First the country begins to "ululate" with the belief that "profit plus regimen equals security" (104). Then the "omnivorous roar" (231) of the Civil War advances the cause of national homogeneity a step further. Finally, twentieth-century technology, in the form of radio, completes the process of assimilation. When the "hollow inverted air" becomes filled with the "resonant boom and ululance of radio," it ceases to be "Yoknapatawpha's air" any longer, or "even Mason and Dixon's" (244). As a result, modern man loses the "last irreconcilable . . . stronghold" from within which he could freely choose "to enter the United States" (246). He has traded his individuality and independence for "one air, one nation: . . . one world: . . . one universe, one cosmos: . . . one swirling rocket-roar filling the glittering zenith as with golden feathers," so that when he now tries to "lift his battered and indomitable head," he finds that "the vast hollow sphere of his air, the vast and terrible burden beneath which he tried to stand erect . . . is murmurous with his fears and terrors and disclaimers and repudiations and his aspirations and dreams and his baseless hopes, bouncing back at him in radar waves from the constellations" (244–247; see Polk 162–163).

This is strong art and prescient social analysis. Although Faulkner was writing before television had had much impact on our culture and well before the portable radio had become an everyday phenomenon, he clearly foresaw both the homogenizing power of the mass media and the impending emergence of a popular culture founded largely on amplified sound, and he developed a powerful array of images with which to express his understanding of these matters. For my purposes here, however, the most important aspect of Faulkner's account of the fall of the modern individual into a world of alien sound is the insight it affords into his view of the situation of the artist—and hence of his own situation—in mid-century America. Underlying this account is a profound antipathy toward American popular culture and an uneasy sense of its threat both to the serious artist in general and to Faulkner himself.

Because Faulkner was a novelist, he was particularly mindful of the threat posed by the aural character of popular culture to the continued preeminence of reading as a cultural activity. He was well aware both of "the density of silence," to use George Steiner's words, "in which the classic exercise of reading took place" ("In a Post-Culture" 159) and of the inroads being made on silence by amplified sound.[14] As he said in an interview in which he explained his preference for prose over music, "music would express better and simpler, but I prefer to use words as I prefer to read rather than listen. I prefer silence to sound, and the image produced by words occurs in silence. That is, the thunder and the music of the prose takes place in silence" (*Lion in the Garden* 248). But in "the patter of comedians, the baritone screams of female vocalists, the babbling pressure to buy and buy and still buy," he foresaw "the last of silence" (*Requiem for a Nun* 244). Because "our culture is production and success," he told an audience in Japan, "folks in the States don't read" (*Lion in the Garden* 90). Hence America, unlike Europe, "has not yet found any place for [the artist] except to use his notoriety to sell soap or cigarettes or fountain pens or to advertise automobiles and cruises and resort hotels, or (if he can be taught to contort fast enough to meet the standards) in radio or moving pictures where he can produce enough income tax to be worth attention" (*Essays* 75). In America, as he once said to Harvey Breit, "the artist is still a little like the old court jester. He's supposed to speak his vicious paradoxes with some sense in them, but he isn't part of whatever the fabric is that makes a nation" (*Lion in the Garden* 82).

This pastiche of quotations could easily be replaced by a different set of the same import, for a sense of the alienated status of the artist in modern America pervades Faulkner's outlook on the world in his later years. One suspects that this attitude would not have surfaced as prominently as it did had Faulkner been able to remain relatively secure in his sense of his own artistic power. He was not, after all, a writer who cared in any conventional way about having an audience, and in such novels as *Pylon* and *The Wild Palms* he had already succeeded in creating art out of American popular culture. But in the 1940s and early 1950s the decline in creativity he had feared finally came about. Time and again during this period, in letters to Joan Williams, Harold Ober, Saxe Commins, and others, Faulkner complains of his growing inability to write and expresses doubt about the staying power of his talent: "what I put down on paper now is not right and I cant get down what I know is right"; "it is getting more and more difficult, a matter of deliberate will power, concentration, which can be deadly after a while"; "I know now that I am getting toward the end, the bottom of the barrel. The stuff is still good, but I know now there is not very much more of it" (*Selected Letters* 344, 345, 348).[15]

Faulkner's sense of the diminishment of his creative power had a complex effect on his postwar fiction and especially on his uses of sound. A proud man, he did not willingly or easily relinquish his belief that he could use his art to give order to the world. Although he expressed self-doubt in his letters, in his fiction he translated his doubt into a doubled effort at interpretation and control. As before, this effort took the form of an attempt to impose his artistic voice on the world's sounds. But here, as in the shift from his early to his mature fiction, continuity is accompanied by significant change. In the fiction of the 1930s, Faulkner had been able to mingle resistance to modernity with regret for the disappearance of an earlier South. But in the postwar period, his diminished confidence in the power of his imagination combined with his sense of alienation to give increased emphasis to resistance alone. In the fiction of this period, the mind and the world struggle with little prospect of reconciliation, only of victory or defeat. As this happens, Faulkner begins to use sound—his characters' voices, his narrative voice, and images of sound as well—in a way that may well remind us of Quentin Compson's use of it in *The Sound and the Fury*: he begins to try to outtalk the world.

This attempt manifests itself in the changed style of the postwar fiction. In a reflective letter to Malcolm Cowley written in 1944, Faulkner points to a link between his style and his relation to the world. "I am telling the same story over and over," he says, "which is myself and the world" (*Selected Letters* 185). After speaking of Thomas Wolfe's effort to put "everything, the world plus 'I' or filtered through 'I' or the effort of 'I' to embrace the world . . . , into one volume," he goes on to say, "I am trying to go a step further. This I think accounts for what people call the obscurity, the involved formless 'style,' endless sentences. I'm trying to say it all in one sentence, between one Cap and one period" (185). Although Faulkner speaks of this effort as if it were uniformly a feature of his fiction throughout his career, it is actually much more characteristic of the style he was evolving at the time he wrote Cowley than of his earlier work. During Faulkner's visit to Japan in 1955, a questioner who was aware of this stylistic change asked Faulkner to explain it. In his reply, which he repeated several times afterwards, Faulkner linked his late predilection for long sentences to his sense of artistic decline and, more generally, to his awareness of his own mortality: "Maybe, as the writer gets old, he realizes that he has [a] shorter and shorter time in which to write before the day comes when he will be tired or will realize that he can't say what he wants to say and so maybe he tries to say all he has not said yet in each sentence, in each paragraph, because maybe he won't live long enough to do another" (*Lion in the Garden* 174–175). In the postwar period, Faulkner's desire to impose artistic order on the world merges with his concern over his ability to continue writing. Out of this merger come the long, accretive, incorporative sentences characteristic of *Intruder in the Dust*, *Requiem for a Nun*, and the other postwar novels.

The richest and most intricate example of a sentence of this sort occurs in "The Jail," the section of *Requiem for a Nun* containing the remarkable image of a "rocket-roar" of noise beating down on the "battered and indomitable head" of modern man. As I suggested, this image is the climax of the depiction of America's fall into noise that threads its way through all three prose sections of the novel. The image is not, however, the climax of "The Jail" itself, for it is embedded deep inside a countermovement designed to annul its power. The agency of this countermovement is the longest sentence—forty-nine pages, twenty-eight paragraphlike sections, and over twelve thousand words—in all of Faulkner's fiction. Together with a thirty-two word introductory sentence, this sentence constitutes the whole of "The Jail." Its extraordinary length alone should suggest something of the significance it holds as an expression of Faulkner's desire to outtalk the world. But to see the full measure of the sentence's significance, we must attend to more than its length, because Faulkner establishes a close congruence between style and theme. The sentence seeks to outtalk the world in duration and also in content; in it, Faulkner depicts an extended act of observation, recollection, writing, and reading that resembles the working of the literary imagination and that results in a final triumphant counterattack of imagined speech on the modern world.

The observer in the sentence is the eponymous hero of the section, the jail itself. For over two-thirds of the sentence's duration, the jail watches as Jefferson eagerly surrenders to the modern world. It is in a position to perform this act of observation because it was bypassed when the "bright rush and roar" of progress "swept the very town one block south" (222) and because it is "insulated by obsolescence" (248). The jail's situation resembles that of "the track-walker in the tunnel, the thunder of the express mounting behind him, who finds himself opposite a niche or crack exactly his size in the wall's living and impregnable rock, and steps into it, inviolable and secure while destruction roars past and on and away" (248). The jail is no merely passive observer, however, for it records what it sees, both literally and mysteriously: literally in "the scrawled illiterate repetitive unimaginative doggerel and the perspectiveless almost prehistoric sexual picture-writing" that lies "invisible and impacted . . . beneath the annual inside creosote-and-whitewash of bullpen and cell," and mysteriously in the power of its "blind outside walls" to absorb and retain, as would a magic mirror, "the images, the panorama . . .

of [the town's] days and years . . . long after the subjects which had reflected the images were vanished and replaced and again replaced" (214–215).

A recording mirror, then, obsolete, located in a backwater, watching the familiar town around it disappear before the ravening advance of modern America, and using the novelist's stock-in-trade of words and images to record its observations: the suspicion grows that we are in the presence of a highly unusual authorial surrogate. This suspicion deepens when we note that in the final third of the section the jail also functions as a text. Inscribed on one of its windows is a statement—"*Cecilia Farmer April 16th 1861*" (229)—that is a synecdochical expression of the whole process of observation and recordkeeping in which the jail has engaged. Like the still, small voice that comes after the wind, earthquake, and fire to guide Elijah, this statement emerges from the "swirling rocket-roar" of modern America's noise to affirm the power of the artist's voice (see Michael Millgate 225; cf. Polk 183–185). It does so by serving as the text for a transformative act of reading. The reader of the inscription is a representative of the modern world whose invasion of Jefferson the jail has watched. He is "a stranger, an outlander say from the East or the North or the Far West" (252), brought to see the incription simply because it is old enough to have become a town relic. At first, because he is ill at ease at "having been dragged without warning or preparation into the private kitchen of a strange woman cooking a meal," the stranger merely looks at the inscription and thinks "*What? So What?*" (254). But then, Faulkner says, speaking of the stranger in the second person, "even while you were thinking it, something has already happened: the faint frail illegible meaningless even inferenceless scratching on the ancient poor-quality glass you stare at, has moved, under your eyes, even while you stared at it, coalesced, seeming actually to have entered into another sense than vision" (254).

Almost in spite of himself, the stranger engages in an act

of reading. He thereby sets in motion a process of the imagination that ultimately annuls not only the modern world's sounds but the very order of reality in which they exist. A reverie occasioned by his act of reading—an exegesis of the text, as it were—brings the outlander to a vision of Cecilia Farmer as "demon-nun and angel-witch; empress, siren, Erinys: Mistinguette, too" (261). This vision, we are told, is "not *might* have been, nor even *could* have been, but *was:* so vast, so limitless in capacity is man's imagination to disperse and burn away the rubble-dross of fact and probability, leaving only truth and dream" (261). Once the stranger arrives at this state of visionary exaltation, the inscription on the window is transformed into imagined speech. When the stranger's act of reading began, Faulkner said that it produced "a scent, a whisper, . . . speaking, murmuring, back from, out of, across from, a time old as lavender, older than album or stereopticon, as old as daguerreotype itself" (254). Now, at the very end of his incredible forty-nine page sentence, Faulkner tells us what the whisper says: out of "a fragile and workless scratching almost depthless in a sheet of old barely transparent glass" emerges "the clear undistanced voice as though out of the delicate antenna-skeins of radio, . . . across the vast instantaneous intervention, from the long long time ago: '*Listen, stranger; this was myself: this was I*'" (261–262).

No greater affirmation exists anywhere in Faulkner's fiction of the power of the artist's voice to overcome the world. His story, he said, was always himself and the world. In "The Jail," he distills the whole long labor of writing that story first into a twelve-thousand-word sentence, then into a twenty-six-character inscription on a jailhouse window, and finally into a self-affirmative statement—"*this was myself: this was I*"—of the sort that he often said lay at the heart of his desire to write. At this climactic moment, the modern world simply ceases to be of any consequence. You, the stranger, Faulkner says, will undoubtedly "unfumble among the road signs and filling stations to get back onto a highway you know, back into the

United States"; but, he continues, "not that it matters, since you know again now that there is no time: no space: no distance" (261). The imagination, acting through the agencies of writing and reading, has annihilated the world of time and space. One may add, as this world vanishes, so does its command over sound, for it is not accidental that in the final clause of his longest sentence Faulkner compares imagined voice to "the delicate antenna-skeins of radio." With this comparison, as he arrogates even the technology of amplified sound itself to the service of the imagination, his long counterattack on the world's noise is finally complete.

Yet we should note that only a battle is won here, not a war, and that the victory comes at no little rhetorical expense. In *A Grammar of Motives,* Kenneth Burke distinguishes between "a calculus of 'therefore,'" as in "God's personality, *therefore* human personality," and "a calculus of 'nevertheless,'" as in "nature's impersonality, *nevertheless* human personality" (112–113). In "The Jail," Faulkner uses an extreme calculus of nevertheless. By filling the first two-thirds of the section with so many hyperbolic images of hostile sound and then circumscribing so severely the subsequent acts of writing, reading, and imagined speech out of which he forms his counterattack, he constructs a worst-case argument for the triumph of art. If a text this slight, a reader initially this indifferent, a speech this short can overcome a world so filled with noise, then surely, he implies the artist's voice can always do so. But the very extremity of this rhetorical strategy at once betrays the uncertainty on which it is founded and inhibits its repeated use. As Faulkner's quick return to images of hostile sound in the nonfiction immediately following *Requiem for a Nun* suggests, he knew, or at least soon learned, that his victory in "The Jail" was only temporary. Yet he also knew, one imagines, that it would be difficult if not impossible to use the drastic strategy of "The Jail" over and over. Hence it is understandable that while he continued to contemplate the modern world and to write long, incorporative sentences, he never again depicted so direct a confrontation between the world's noise and the artist's voice.[16]

IV

Faulkner instead turned to silence, seeking in it both retreat from the world and an alternative strategy of artistic control. He thereby put to new use images and ideas of long-standing interest to him, for silence always occupied an important place in his fiction. From the beginning of his career, Faulkner expressed his yearning for reconciliation with the world almost as often in images of silence as in images of sound. In *The Marble Faun*, for example, "Warmth and Peace go hand in hand/'Neath Silence's inverted eyes" (22); and in the "hushed pool" beside which Pan "stays and broods" can be seen reflected "His own face and the bending sky/In shivering soundless amity" (16). As with these images of reconciliation, so also with their overthrow, for like sound, silence is always liable in Faulkner's fiction to invasion by noise. Thus, in *Flags in the Dust*, the "walled serene tower of his deafness" that permits the elder Bayard Sartoris to exist in a condition of "rapt imperturbability" (37) is unable to hold out the "warning thunder" (92) of his grandson's car and of the modern age it symbolizes; and in *Sanctuary*, in another image of the violation of silence by a representative of the modern age, Temple Drake imagines in the moment just before her rape that "sound and silence had become inverted," so that "she could hear silence in a thick rustling as [Popeye] moved toward her through it, thrusting it aside" (99).

One of the main ways Faulkner envisioned silence in his early career was as an antecedent to speech. In the 1920s, as Paul Lilly shows, Faulkner borrowed from the French symbolists the belief that all artistic expression is a betrayal into speech of ineffable emotions. Silence was for him an ideal condition, a paradisaical state out of which one falls into the imperfection of language; and in another sense it was the source of narrative itself, for time and again in his fiction Faulkner attributes talismanic significance to a silent or absent character, whose meaning and value he then attempts to recover through an act of narration. But as his career advanced, the conditions I have been discussing—the growing volume of the world's noise, his sense of his own declining artistic power—caused Faulkner gradually to shift his focus from silence as the source of speech to silence as its goal. In the letters and public statements of the postwar period, he repeatedly expresses a desire either to withdraw into silence or to impose silence on the outside world. He fantasizes that it might be possible to "anesthetize, for one year, American vocal chords [sic]"; he says that he would like to be free of "the curse of human speech"; and he threatens, half-humorously and yet half-seriously, to "break the pencil" and to lapse into silence (*Selected Letters* 234, 251–252, 404, 424–425; *Lion in the Garden* 255).

In all his comments about retreating into silence, Faulkner speaks as if it were an act innocent of public meaning, a purely private response to internal needs. Yet clearly for him to have lapsed into silence would have constituted a message to the world. "Silence" is a relative term, not an absolute one: like "left" and "right" and "near" and "far," "silence" and "sound" define each other. Faulkner's silence would necessarily have existed in the context of his previous encounters with the world and would have formed a comment on them. This is especially so because in the twentieth century silence has become a limit term in the rhetoric of artistic alienation. As Susan Sontag argues in *Styles of Radical Will*, such figures as Arthur Rimbaud, Marcel Duchamp, and J. D. Salinger exemplify a distinctively modern tradition of significant withdrawal into silence. In the decision of these and other artists to cease producing art, "one cannot fail to perceive," as Sontag says, ". . . a highly social gesture" (6). This gesture can only be made by an artist who "has demonstrated that he possesses genius and [who has] exercised that genius authoritatively" (7). For such a person, the deliberate withdrawal into silence becomes an indictment of the world for its inadequacy, both as audience and as object of aesthetic contemplation (cf. Steiner, "Silence and the Poet").[17]

Yet, as Sontag also says, "the exemplary modern artist's choice of silence is rarely carried to this point of final simplification, so that he becomes literally silent" (7). This is so, one suspects, because the uncompromising rigor of a full retreat into silence, although rhetorical, runs fundamentally counter to the artist's basic enterprise: it allows no room for reshaping, qualifying, or elaborating one's meaning or for correcting misinterpretations. Whether for this reason or for another, Faulkner's dream of withdrawing into silence was never destined to be acted on in its own form. Instead, for him, as for a number of other artists (e.g., Beckett), silence served as a stimulus to further creativity. By turning his fiction back on his desire to become silent—and, alternatively, on his desire to impose silence on the world—Faulkner created a kind of boundary art, making speech out of his desire to be free of speech and thereby regaining the ability to give order to the world.

The two postwar novels in which Faulkner most fully expresses his interest in silence are *A Fable* and *The Mansion.* In the first, he focuses on a source of silence; in the second, on a casualty of sound. As is well known, *A Fable* had its origin in the idea of treating the unknown soldier as if he were Christ come to earth again. This idea, central as it is to Faulkner's meaning, seems to have commanded his imagination less than did the opportunity to explore the rhetoric of silence. The historical germ of this exploration is a highly symbolic moment of silence that occurred at the end of World War I. Although the armistice that suspended hostilities was signed at 5:30 A.M. on 11 November 1918, it did not go into effect until 11:00 A.M. the same day. This delay, said to have been occasioned by a desire to have the hostilities cease at the eleventh hour of the eleventh day of the eleventh month, created a dramatic moment of silence, for it allowed the great guns on both sides of the front to cease firing at exactly the same time. Coming after more than four years of nearly continual bombardment, this sudden silence left such an indelible impression on the people present that it rapidly became part of the folklore of the war; it receives prominent mention in many postwar memoirs, poems, and works of fiction, and it was memorialized by a ritual observance of silence in the Armistice Day ceremonies of all the major allied countries.[18]

In *A Fable*, Faulkner adapts the sudden silencing of the guns to his purposes by making it the main effect of the Corporal's refusal to charge. We are told repeatedly that the mutiny of the Corporal and his comrades has imposed silence on the world: "Silence, falling suddenly out of the sky on the human race"; "ringing silence"; "unbearable golden silence"; "silence . . . falling like a millstone into a well" (11, 37, 93). By shifting control over the sound of the guns from the generals and politicians who possessed it in the real war to his fictional Corporal, Faulkner converts the Corporal's inaction into a form of speech. This effect arises not only from the mutiny itself but from the Corporal's disinclination to talk about it afterwards. By first refusing to fight and then failing to explain his reasons for doing so, the Corporal creates a rhetoric of silence, one powerful enough to make all western Europe his mute and attentive audience. Through the eloquence of his silence, he elicits the world's silence in response.

The central task that the Corporal faces in the course of the novel is to maintain faith in the efficacy of his silence. At issue in the climactic confrontation between the Corporal and the Old General on the eve of the Corporal's execution is both the message and the method of the Corporal's rhetoric. As the Old General says, he and the Corporal "are two articulations, self-elected possibly, anyway elected, anyway postulated, not so much to defend as to test two inimical conditions: . . . I champion of this mundane earth; . . . you champion of an esoteric realm of man's baseless hopes and his infinite capacity—

no: passion—for unfact" (347–348). Although the General's statement emphasizes his and the Corporal's differing beliefs, it should be clear that the two of them are also opposed "articulations" in the sense that they embody two different styles of discourse, with the General's verbosity standing in polar opposition to the Corporal's taciturnity and reliance on symbolic gesture.

Understandably, then, the General seeks not only to annul the meaning of the Corporal's mutiny but also to substitute for the Corporal's faith in silence a belief in sound. This he does when he tempts the Corporal for the third and final time. After the Corporal quickly rejects the General's offers of freedom and power, the General turns to his last temptation, saying "then take life" (350) and telling the story of the condemned man and the bird. This man, the General says, recanted his confession at the moment of his hanging because a bird lighted on the only tree limb visible from the gallows "and opened its tiny throat and sang" (351). The bird's song, the General suggests, expresses the sweetness of life on "this mundane earth" (348). Although in itself the bird is a "weightless and ephemeral creature which hawk might stoop at or snare or lime or random pellet of some idle boy destroy," always "there would be another bird, another spring, the same bough leafed again and another bird to sing on it, if [the condemned man] is only here to hear it, can only remain" (351). "Take that bird" (351) the General says to the Corporal. "Recant, confess, say you were wrong. . . . Close the window upon that baseless dream. Open this other one [where] . . . that single bough . . . will be there always waiting and ready for that weightless and ephemeral burden. Take that bird" (351–352).

The Corporal rejects this temptation as quickly and easily as he did the other two. As Irving Howe suggests, the ease with which the Corporal resists all of the General's temptations reveals Faulkner's underlying assumption that his characters "are reenacting a great drama and must, therefore, abide by its fated patterns" (272). Viewed from the perspective I offer here, the ease of the Corporal's resistance also reveals Faulkner's disinterest at this stage in his career in assigning the same imaginative authority to the dream of union with the world as to the dream of silence. Certainly his argument in favor of such a union lacks evocative power. Although he takes pains to locate the anecdote of the hanged man in Mississippi, the bird he uses to exemplify the richness of life in the mundane world owes far more allegiance to Keats's nightingale than to the birds of his native region. It is as if the Carolina wrens and mockingbirds and "the big woodpecker called Lord-to-God by negroes" (*Go Down, Moses* 202) with which Faulkner had populated the fiction of his great middle phase had faded into inaudibility, leaving behind only an argument for union with the world as abstract and literary in its contours as were the ones he advanced at the beginning of his career.

It is scarcely surprising, then, that the Corporal chooses to maintain his allegiance to silence. He thereby ensures that he will become enclosed in silence ever more completely, for when he descends from the mountain his fated pattern carries him first back to prison, then to execution, then to burial, and finally to entombment beneath the cenotaph commemorating the unknown dead. But even in the Corporal's final immurement we see enacted Faulkner's dream of a muteness replete with meaning. At the end of the novel, the General is brought back into conjunction with the Corporal when the caisson bearing the General's dead body is placed before the cenotaph in preparation for his funeral. The attitudes toward sound and silence that the General and the Corporal had embodied in life also are brought into conjunction once more, this time through the surrogate figures of the Battalion Runner and the statesman who plans to deliver the General's funeral oration. Because the Runner remembers the Corporal's gesture of silent refusal—because he still hears it, as it were—he has no tolerance for "the orator's voice ringing now into the grieving circumambience" (435) but instead disrupts the service and stops the speech. This gesture symbolically vindicates the Corporal's faith in the efficacy of his silence: as the Battalion Runner takes on the mantle of discipleship, the dead Corporal's silence emerges from the tomb and again imposes silence on the world.

The basic situation of *A Fable* bears a resemblance to that of "The Jail," where Faulkner also depicts meaning as entrapped or imprisoned. In both works, too, the release of meaning from its imprisonment is not entirely within the power of its creator to effect but instead requires the cooperation of a willing reader (or listener). In depicting the liberation of meaning as depending on an interaction between reader and text, Faulkner memorializes his own earlier fictional practice, for in such novels as *Absalom, Absalom!* and *Go Down, Moses,* he often places his characters in situations where they must engage in creative acts of reading and listening, and he often devises fictional structures that invite his readers to share in the process. In the context of the late fiction, this sort of reader-text interaction has an anachronistic air, because by this point in his career, Faulkner has shifted to a more didactic—or at least more explicit—model for fictional meaning. In *The Mansion,* in the last significant exploration of either sound or silence that he ever made, Faulkner depicts the reader-text relation in a way more consistent with his postwar fictional practice. He does so by deafening Linda Snopes Kohl.

Along with Charles Mallison, her companion character in *The Town* and *The Mansion,* Linda Snopes Kohl is almost the only sympathetically depicted character in Faulkner's fiction whose date of birth falls after the turn of the century. By sending her to Greenwich Village, marrying her to "a liberal emancipated advanced-thinking artist," having her become a Communist and fight in the Spanish Civil War, and finally returning her to Jefferson to struggle for "the liberation [of humanity] at last and forever from pain and hunger and injustice," Faulkner makes her his fullest fictional embodiment of the modern liberal spirit (*The Mansion* 164, 222). But she lacks one of that spirit's defining characteristics. Because her deafness has left her with "that dry harsh quacking voice that deaf people learn to use" (199), she seldom speaks, and then almost always only in response to other people's comments and questions. She is the spirit of the modern age revised in one crucial aspect: she is silent.[19]

By thus imposing silence on the modern world, Faulkner engages in a direct, almost brutal form of artistic control. Because Linda so seldom speaks, she is essentially deprived of the ability to explain her own actions: like the Corporal in *A Fable*, she is a mute signifier, a silent text awaiting elucidation. Faulkner's attitude toward her silence, however, differs significantly from his attitude toward that of the Corporal. Because the Corporal's alienation from the world around him resembles Faulkner's own, Faulkner's engagement with silence in *A Fable* is primarily interpretative: his task, as he sees it, is to elicit and display the meaning concealed within the Corporal's muteness. But because Linda embodies the modern world of which he was so critical, Faulkner views her less as a text to be interpreted than as one to be rewritten. In effect, he uses her silence as a new kind of counterattack on the world; by deafening her, he places the world in a position where it can be reconstituted in a form more consistent with his own values and beliefs. He does this in two ways: by extracting Linda from her involvement in the dialectic of modern history and returning her to the timeless world of myth and by substituting Gavin Stevens's voice for Linda's at crucial points in the text.

Of the three named narrators in *The Mansion*, the one who is most aware that Linda's return to Jefferson provides an opportunity for an act of rewriting is Charles Mallison. He suggests the need for a redefinition of her meaning in his repeated emphasis on the incongruity, from Jefferson's standpoint, of viewing her as "a wounded female war veteran" (109). As he says ironically, while waiting at the Memphis airport for her flight to arrive, "you would think the whole town would turn out, or at least be represented by delegates: . . . which would have happened if she had been elected Miss America instead of merely blown up by a Franco shell or land mine or whatever it was" (192). Linda's identity as a war hero exists only in the frame of values of the world from which she is returning; to Jefferson, the designation is incomprehensible. Yet no alternative identity is immediately available. Interdicted by her ideology and her cosmopolitan experiences from the bourgeois society of the Jefferson women of her own age, she seems to Mallison equally incapable of being assimilated to the mythic world in which her mother had resided. On the one hand, he asks rhetorically, "what would she want in a Ladies' Auxiliary, raffling off homemade jam and lamp shades" (192); yet on the other hand, that "aura, nimbus, condition" that had made her mother a modern-day equivalent of Helen of Troy and Venus clearly "was not transferable" (211–212).

In Linda's deafness Mallison discovers a way to remove her from history and return her to myth. He ascribes this redefinition of her meaning to his uncle. For Gavin Stevens, Mallison suggests, the significance of Linda's deafness lies in its ability to annul her sexuality and, more generally, her capacity to change in time. Mallison arrives at this insight by reflecting on how Linda differs from the other young girls in whom Stevens had displayed an avuncular interest. "The other times," he says, "[the girls] had flicked the skirt or flowed or turned the limb at and into mere puberty" (203). When this happened, Stevens lost interest in them, for beyond puberty "was the other door immediately beyond which was the altar and the long line of drying diapers: fulfillment, the end" (203). But after her deafening, Linda is no longer "in motion continuous through a door" but is instead " . . . herself the immobile one while it was the door and the walls it opened which fled away and on" (203). Deafened, Linda becomes an "inviolate bride of silence, inviolable in maidenhead, fixed, forever safe from change and alteration" (203).

In the allusion to Keats's "Ode on a Grecian Urn" that he makes here and repeats elsewhere, Mallison suggests the mythic role that Linda's silence engenders for her: although clearly no goddess of love, Linda can nonetheless serve, like Keats's bride of quietness, as a tutelary deity for the dream of a life free of time.[20] This mythic identity is directly opposed to the dialectical view of time implicit in Linda's belief in communism and in her role as a representative of the modern age. By redefining Linda in this way, Mallison and his companions are able to assimilate her beliefs to their own. She is "doomed," Ratliff says, " . . . to love once quick and lose him quick and for the rest of her life to be faithful and to grieve" (158), and he, Stevens, and Mallison tirelessly interpret and reinterpret her actions and attitudes until they can be made to bear meanings consistent with this view of her as a fated victim. Thus her allegiance to communism, far from being a sign of her immersion in time, becomes for them a reflex of her fixed and undying grief: only because the Communist Party has "already proved itself immune to bullets and therefore immortal" (233), Stevens says, does Linda continue to believe in it, for what she truly seeks from it is not involvement in the political life of her age but a way of forever remembering her dead husband.

The second form of Faulkner's attempt to confine the modern world within the Procrustean bed of his art follows almost inevitably from the first. Lauded for silence, uncomfortable in speech, Linda quite naturally accedes to Stevens's inclination to replace her voice with his own. As she does, the system of beliefs she represents recedes further into the background. It is significant, for example, that Faulkner chooses to have Gihon, the FBI agent, speak to Stevens rather than to Linda, for he thereby converts what could have been a symbolic confrontation between communism and an American approximation of fascism into an opportunity for Stevens to affirm the primacy of personal loyalty over more remote allegiances. In the larger action of the novel, a similar transformation takes place, for the potential battle between Linda's communism and Flem's capitalism undergoes substantial redefinition when it is filtered through Stevens's mind and voice. Far from seeing the events preceding Flem's death as a struggle between the two great value systems of the modern world, Stevens works assiduously to protect Linda from all knowledge of what is happening, as if he thought of her as a helpless southern maiden and of himself as her knightly protector. And when Stevens reflects on his actions, he continues this process of displacement, by using philosophical and moral categories, not political ones, to analyze his experiences. He is eager, for example, to learn whether Mink's release from prison will confirm his long-standing belief in "fate and destiny" (368), and he repeatedly wonders whether his hope that "*none of it will spatter on me*" (376) means that he is a moral coward.

By silencing Linda, Faulkner remakes the modern world into a feasible subject for his art. Along with this rehabilitation of the world as subject comes a rehabilitation of it as audience, for by deafening Linda, Faulkner forces the world to abandon its allegiance to sound and to resume its commitment to reading. He emphasizes this change by having Gavin Stevens give Linda a gift of "a little pad of thin ivory leaves just about big enough to hold three words at a time" (216) and by repeatedly depicting the two of them engaging in written conversations. He thereby constructs an image of reading as an almost totally dependent process. Linda, we may recall, had always been guided in her reading by Stevens, for according to Ratliff, Stevens "had been giving [her] books to read ever since she was fourteen and then kind of holding examinations on them" (138). The reading Linda does after her deafening lacks even the slight degree of independence found in this system of assignments and examinations: as Stevens says, she now reads "the words as my hand formed them, like speech, almost like hearing" (237). By depriving Linda of the solitude in which the act of reading typically takes place, Faulkner places Stevens in a position of almost total control over the creation of meaning. Stevens knows immediately whether his words are having the desired effect, and, if they are not, he revises them, rewrites them, makes them larger and more insistent, until at last Linda accedes to their power and either believes or acts as he wishes.[21]

In depicting this seeming dependence of reader on writer, Faulkner brings his final counterattack on the modern world momentarily to victory. One imagines that he must have taken considerable delight in devising an image for the act of reading that annihilates so completely the world's allegiance to sound and that returns the writer and the writer's art so fully to a position of cultural dominance. Yet this dream of a world transformed into the shape of the writer's desire, entrancing though it must have been, could not long survive the candor with which Faulkner understood the situation of the artist in the modern world. Although Stevens appears to have enclosed the world inside a net of writing, at the last it escapes. By placing an order for a new automobile immediately after she has become convinced that Stevens will be able to secure Mink's release, Linda demonstrates, as Ratliff says, that "she knowed all the time what was going to happen when he got out" (431). She thus engages in an act of silent communication that renders her entirely and forever free from Stevens's desperate efforts to enclose her inside the "rational garrulity of the pencil flying along the ruled lines" (371).

Considered from the point of view I am advancing here, the situation Linda creates by her gesture has considerable poignancy. After she has engaged in her act of silent communication, she returns to New York, the center of the world she symbolizes and the place that is now her rightful home. She leaves behind "two old men . . . approaching their sixties" (434), one of whom—Stevens—weeps as he desperately tries to deny the significance of her action: "I wont believe it! . . . I wont! I cant believe it. . . . Dont you see I cannot?" (431). For Stevens, and surely, one imagines, for Faulkner himself, the failure to enclose the world inside writing is an occasion for grief. Yet one must not insist too strongly on the identification here between author and character, for it ultimately breaks down, as it always must: Stevens weeps, but Faulkner writes about his weeping—and then moves on to yet one more rendition of the dream of reconciliation with the world, when he describes Mink Snopes "beginning to creep, seep, flow easy as sleeping . . . down and down into the ground" (435). What we are left with at the end of *The Mansion*, then, and at the end of his long encounter with sound, is an image of Faulkner perhaps less poignant than the image of Stevens weeping but more true: not entirely Stevens, neither is he entirely Mink Snopes; he is a writer, alone with his voice, making art out of absence.

TWO

The Root of All Evil

Throughout his career, William Faulkner tended to downplay any suggestion that his experiences in Hollywood had significantly influenced his serious fiction. In both his letters and his public statements and interviews, he depicted his work in Hollywood as an unpleasant necessity, a form of prostitution, something from which he needed to recover before turning to serious writing, but never as either source or subject for his art.[1] If we limit our attention to acts of direct representation, then Faulkner's attitude is certainly understandable, for with the exception of the story "Golden Land," he never uses a Hollywood setting in his fiction. But if we broaden our scope to include indirect as well as direct representations, then we arrive at a considerably different conclusion. Twice in the 1930s, Faulkner wrote novels depicting in a parabolic fashion the circumstances to which he was exposed during his sojourns in Hollywood. The two novels are *Pylon* and *The Wild Palms*. In both, Faulkner meditates intensely on the implications for his fiction and for his life as an artist of the world of wage labor and commercial art.

Central to both these meditations is the theme of money. *Pylon* begins with the mechanic, Jiggs, haggling with a pair of store clerks to reduce the down payment on a pair of boots from $2.25 to $2.10; it ends with the reporter demanding, via a note, that his editor "*bring* [him] *some jack*" (315). Between these points, the novel depicts, by a conservative estimate, over sixty separate financial transactions, ranging in size from a ten-cent loan to the would-be purchase of Matt Ord's airplane for $5000. Similarly, as Thomas McHaney has shown,

Faulkner traces Harry Wilbourne and Charlotte Rittenmeyer's shifting financial fortunes in *The Wild Palms* in such detail that we frequently know to the dollar the amount of money they possess (*William Faulkner's "The Wild Palms"* 204–206). These representations, so extensive as to constitute a dominant theme in both novels, resonate against each other in intriguing ways, as if Faulkner had decided in *The Wild Palms* to extend and deepen a line of thought he had begun but not completed in *Pylon*. Moreover, Faulkner's exploration of the theme of money exposes the more complex and abiding theme of his attitude toward material existence itself; and the way this theme is developed both intensifies and renders problematic his association of his artistic identity with the South. Examining the role of money in *Pylon* and *The Wild Palms,* then, should add not only to our appreciation of the two novels considered separately but to our understanding of the place they occupy in the development of Faulkner's artistic vision.

I

Faulkner suggests a primary meaning that he attributes to money early in *Pylon,* in the text of the dedicatory plaque of Feinman Airport:

FEINMAN AIRPORT

NEW VALOIS, FRANCIANA

DEDICATED TO

THE AVIATORS OF AMERICA

AND

COLONEL H. I. FEINMAN, CHAIRMAN

SEWAGE BOARD

Through Whose Undeviating Vision and Unflagging Effort
This Airport was Raised Up and Created out of the
Waste Land at the Bottom of Lake Rambaud at a Cost
of One Million Dollars (14).

The collocation here of sewage board, waste land, and money introduces a central element of the novel's vision of life. On almost every page, *Pylon* assaults us with an array of visceral and excremental images and references. Colonel Feinman is twice referred to as "General Behindman," a double-edged allusion to his role on the sewage board and to the delay the barnstormers experience in receiving their prize money; the debris left behind by the Mardi Gras is called "tinseldung"; an ashtray in a hotel lobby is called a "Basque chamberpot" on one occasion and a "greaser chamberpot" on another; Laverne does not wear underpants on the occasion of her first parachute jump out of fear that she will befoul them; Roger invites Jiggs to bathe in a slop jar; the reporter sleeps in vomit. This list of examples could easily be extended, but doing so would merely confirm what should already be evident: that central to *Pylon* is an oppressive, emotion-laden awareness of the cloacal side of human experience.

Poised against this nightmare vision of a world dominated by "the secret implacable eyeless life of [the] entrails," as Faulkner elsewhere calls it (*Collected Stories* 640) is the novel's romance of the air. In organizing *Pylon* around a contrast between air and excrement—or, more broadly, between air and earth, motion and matter—Faulkner invokes one of the central symbolic oppositions of his fiction. Nowhere does he imbue this opposition with a sharper emotional contrast than here, for throughout *Pylon* he repeatedly associates air, sky, and motion with life, and earth, excrement, and stasis with death. This is true dramatically as well as symbolically and imagistically, for the romantic attractiveness of the barnstormers (in contrast to the earthbound characters of the novel) lies largely in their allegiance to motion and their resistance to matter. As in the instance of Laverne Shumann's frantic act of lovemaking before her parachute jump, the barnstormers' flights are death-defying in a literal sense of the term. They are attempts to rise above this "puny crawling painwebbed globe" (28) and to deny the inevitability of its claim on their existence.

The main action of *Pylon* consists of the defeat of these attempts, both directly, in the experience of the barnstormers themselves, and indirectly, in the experience of the reporter. Central to this action in both its forms is money, which Faulkner depicts as possessing an extraordinarily destructive power. This power arises in part from the circumstances in which the barnstormers find themselves. As Faulkner said many years later, "there was really no place for [the barnstormers] in the culture, in the economy" (*Faulkner in the University* 36); thus, they are subject to exploitation by Colonel Feinman and by others in positions of power and privilege.[2] But Faulkner's depiction of the destructive power of money in *Pylon* is ultimately less economic than existential. He links money with death, as he links excrement with death, because both symbolize the barnstormers' unavoidable implication in the material world. In Roger Shumann's death scene, Faulkner depicts this three-way linkage allegorically. Needing money to meet the expenses of Laverne's pregnancy and to replace his damaged aircraft, Roger chooses to race the plane he and the reporter have surreptitiously "purchased" from Matt Ord. In an attempt to stabilize the craft, Roger places a sandbag in the rear of the fuselage. When he chooses to compete for first place and its greater prize money, rather than fly safely and finish second, the sandbag breaks loose, and the sand emerges from the rear of the plane in a grotesque mechanical parody of excretion, appearing first as "a light scattering of burnt paper or feathers," then as "a whole wastebasketful of the light trash" (234). Then when the craft plummets into Lake Rambaud, Faulkner makes clear the symbolic significance of the entire episode by saying that the plane and Roger's body both lodge irrecoverably in "a sunken mole composed of refuse from the city itself—shards of condemned paving and masses of fallen walls and even discarded automobile bodies—any and all the refuse of man's twentieth century clotting into communities large enough to pay a mayor's salary" (236–237).[3]

Faulkner's use of the barnstormers to create a stark portrait of the degrading and life-destroying power of the need for money extends far beyond his depiction of Roger Shumann's death, into almost every aspect of the barnstormers' career in the novel. One thinks, for example, of their pathetic attempts to maintain dignity while filching money from the reporter's pockets, and of the grim scene of Laverne and Roger standing in the lobby of a hotel they cannot afford to sleep in, waiting for the beds they have rented in a brothel to empty for the night. The intensity of this portrait results in large measure from its single-mindedness. It is a fully externalized indictment of the power of money, a demonstration of its ability to victimize even those people who try to live as if it did not matter. In the story of the reporter, Faulkner internalizes this indictment, by exploring the capacity of money to degrade not only the circumstances but also the mind of a character. He thereby begins an examination of the psychology of money to which he returns in a fuller and more complex way in his portrait of Harry Wilbourne in *The Wild Palms*.

The reporter's tragedy, if it may be termed that, consists in his being a barnstormer *manqué*. In a number of ways—his vicarious participation in the air races, his attempt to learn to fly himself, even his relative weightlessness—the reporter exhibits his desire to transcend material existence and enter the realm of pure motion. His improvident expenditure of money also expresses this desire, for it is so frequent and so extreme as to constitute a symbolic attempt to divest himself of his material being. Yet in contrast to the barnstormers, whose insolvency is unrelentingly authentic, the reporter's financial embarrassments exude an air of childlike make-believe. Supported by a salary, by his mother's gifts, and by Hagood's exasperated but apparently unlimited generosity, the reporter merely plays at imitating the financial condition of the barnstormers.[4] More important, his expenditures are duplicitous in another way, for he does not, as he pretends, spend money on the barnstormers for purely altruistic reasons. As the barnstormers all realize, he is trying to buy his way into their world. Like the spectators at the air show, only more emphatically, the reporter gives the barnstormers money in exchange for vicarious access to their adventures.

Discovering the underlying duplicity in his relation with the barnstormers is the reporter's one positive achievement in the course of the novel; but by its nature, this achievement offers him no comfort, instead reducing him to a condition of death-in-life symbolically equivalent to Roger's actual death. The reporter enters this condition in two stages, the first of which consists of a despairing realization of the impossibility of the dream of pure motion. The ecstasy the reporter feels in helping Roger test Matt Ord's aircraft results from the peculiarity of his physical posture during the flight. Lying on his stomach in the womblike fuselage, incapable of seeing the outside world, the reporter experiences a "blind timeless period . . . of . . . terrific motion—not speed and not progress—just blind furious motion" (216–217). Riding out to the airport after the barnstormers' departure from New Valois, he starts to experience this sensation again, as a result "of being suspended in a small airtight glass box clinging by two puny fingers of light in the silent and rushing immensity of space" (283). When he notices how the light from the city parallels his movement, "regardless at what terrific speed and in what loneliness," he understands for the first time the inescapability of the material world—how, "symbolic and encompassing, [the light] outlay all gasolinespanned distances and all clock- or sun-stipulated destinations" (283–284). He then broods on his future in relation to this world, a future which he envisions as an undesirable but unavoidable immersion in the physical sensations of the city: "the eternal smell of the coffee the sugar the hemp sweating slow . . . the myriad fish stewed in a myriad oil [for] tomorrow and tomorrow and tomorrow; not only not to hope, not even to wait: just to endure" (284).

Despairing as this vision is, it gives way to an even deeper despair when the reporter realizes the significance of the $175 he placed in Jack Shumann's toy airplane. From the time Roger Shumann dies until almost the end of the novel, the reporter denies—even to himself—that he had any ulterior motive in urging Roger to fly Matt Ord's aircraft. But when he learns that Laverne and Jack Holmes have gone to Ohio to leave Jack Shumann with Roger's parents and that therefore the trio will not remain intact, his psychological defenses collapse. Placing the money in the toy airplane parodically repeats the $5000 purchase, in that the reporter puts the money in the toy, as he had helped buy the airplane, out of his desire to become a member of the barnstormers' odd ménage. As he says, "I just thought . . . that maybe the hundred and seventy-five would be enough until Holmes could . . . and that then [Jack] would be big enough and I would be there" (301; second ellipsis Faulkner's). Learning that his fantasy of reunion will never be realized forces the reporter to understand that his lavishing of money on the barnstormers was not as disinterested as he had pretended. Faced with this realization, he enacts a psychological equivalent of Roger's descent into the lake, first by imagining himself "having to lie there too and look up at the wreath dissolving," and then by experiencing the alcohol he is drinking as "so much dead icy water, cold and heavy and lifeless in his stomach" (301–302). There is little reason to believe that he will ever recover from this descent. Bereft of both self-delusion and hope, his future promises only a series of caustic reenactments of his simultaneous repudiation of, and reliance on, money: "*I am going down to Amboise st. and get drunk . . . and if you dont know what drunk is come down there and look at me and when you come bring some jack because I am on a credit*" (315).

II

As with so many of Faulkner's novels, *Pylon* gains in significance when viewed in relation to his career. The novel most obviously reflects Faulkner's life in the use it makes of events he observed during the dedication of Shushan Airport in New Orleans in February, 1934—a use so extensive as to cause him to warn his publisher of the possibility of a suit for libel (*Selected Letters* 86–87).[5] But these correspondences, intriguing as they are, will mislead us if they cause us to view *Pylon* as merely "the outcome," in Judith Bryant Wittenberg's words, "of an interest that was, so to speak, extracurricular" and hence as "peripheral to . . . the essential man" (131). If we are to see the novel's biographical significance in a fuller way, we need to move beyond its direct representation of Faulkner's experiences to the way it reconstitutes those experiences at the level of theme and vision. Viewed in this way, *Pylon* reveals its relation to Faulkner's life to lie less in his "extracurricular" interest in barnstorming than in changes occurring in his understanding of himself as an economic being.

These changes were far-reaching and profound. In the 1920s, an insouciant attitude toward money and a willingness to support himself by a variety of odd jobs were both prominent parts of Faulkner's bohemian artistic self-conception.[6] But by the mid-1930s, Faulkner had become a husband, a stepfather, a father, and the mortgagor of a substantial piece of real estate. With these changes came a familiar sort of change in his attitude toward money; as he said in a letter written in 1932, "I am not young enough anymore to hell around and earn money at other things as I could once. I have got to make it by writing or quit writing" (*Selected Letters* 60). Yet as he soon learned, he could neither "make it" by writing—at least not by writing serious fiction alone—nor quit. Hence his earlier insouciance disappeared, to be replaced by periodic trips to Hollywood (the second of which occurred the summer before he wrote *Pylon*) and by an anxiety about money that was to dog him intermittently for the next fifteen years. Accompanying these changes was a sense of their incompatibility with his role as a serious artist: as he said in another letter, written to his agent shortly after he had completed *Pylon,* "I cannot and will not go on like this. I believe I have got enough fair literature in me yet to deserve reasonable freedom from bourgeoise [sic] material petty impediments and compulsion [sic], without having to quit writing and go to the moving pictures every two years" (*Selected Letters* 90).[7]

In the reporter's career as a journalist, we see an exaggerated version of these frustrations and anxieties. Despite his emotional and financial dependence on Hagood and his near-obsession with buying newspapers, the reporter is profoundly disenchanted with the world of journalism. This disenchantment springs in part from his sense of the compromises inherent in the medium; as he says to Hagood, with characteristic vehemence, he and the other reporters must "run our ass ragged between what Grandlieu Street kikes tell us to print in their half of the paper and tell you what you can't print in our half and still find something to fill the blank spaces under Connotator of the World's Doings and Moulder of the Peoples' Thought" (65). A deeper source of the reporter's disaffection, though, is the antagonistic relation journalism bears to the dream of transcendence symbolized by the barnstormers. A newspaper, the narrator says, is "the dead instant's fruit of forty tons of machinery and an entire nation's antic delusion" (111). Although the nature of this "antic delusion" is never specified, clearly it consists in the belief that life (in the sense of motion) can be captured and experienced vicariously. If we add to this observation an awareness of the extraordinary extent to which Faulkner depicts newspapers as material entities rather than as carriers of meaning—the "thick heavy typesplattered" (13) pages, the "black bold stilldamp" (42) print—then we see that journalism is another form of the imprisoning corruption into which the dream of pure motion is doomed to descend. By telling the story of the barnstormers in a way that will sell—"Burnham Burns"—the reporter and his colleagues engage in a verbal equivalent of Roger's descent into the mire.

The nature of the reporter's disenchantment with journalism suggests obvious parallels to Faulkner's attitude toward writing for the movies—both to his sense that "a moving picture is by its nature a collaboration and any collaboration is compromise" (*Lion in the Garden* 240) and to his more general sense of the threat posed to serious literature by the popular media. The reporter's career as a writer parallels Faulkner's in another way, too, for the reporter is apparently an aspiring novelist; he is enough of one, at least, to need to be told by Hagood that the newspaper has no room for "Lewises or Hemingways or even Tchekovs on the staff" (50). Understandably, then, he is moved by an impulse to give his experiences with the barnstormers a more worthy verbal embodiment than journalism will allow. This he attempts to do during the time between his discovery of his partial responsibility for Roger's death and his departure for Amboise Street, by beginning an account of the wreathlaying that the copyboy believes "to be not only news but the beginning of literature" (314). This attempt is frustrated by the reporter's obligation to report the news in the way Hagood wants and the public demands; yet his attempt to recount the event journalistically is also frustrated, for his disgust at converting the experience into newspaper copy breaks through in almost every phrase of the account he leaves on Hagood's desk. His two ways of writing are thus mutually destructive, as Faulkner must at times have imagined his own to be: the need to write for hire undermining serious art, the desire to create serious art undermining writing for hire.

III

Read as I have read it here, *Pylon* reveals itself to be a reflection on the emotional and artistic dangers arising from the need for money. Most students of Faulkner would agree that a desire to remain free of an excessive dependence on money was an enduring aspect of his character. But the intensity with which Faulkner repudiates money in *Pylon,* while clearly suited to his mood at the moment, threatens to obscure an important dimension of his artistic vision. By associating money with the material world and repudiating both, Faulkner ignores a deeply materialistic strain in his own thought. Here I am not speaking of materialism as acquisitiveness but as a philosophy—specifically, as the belief that ideas have no existence independent of their material manifestations.[8] Faulkner often displays his sympathy with this belief. It appears in both his fiction and his non-fiction in a variety of forms, such as his rejection of belief in an afterlife and in the existence of an immaterial soul; perhaps its most familiar manifestation is the assertion, which appears first in *Mosquitoes* and reappears in *Absalom, Absalom!* and *The Wild Palms,* that memory is a condition of the muscles rather than of the mind.

This materialistic strain in Faulkner's thought creates a need for an alternative to the point of view expressed in *Pylon.* The extreme body-spirit dualism of *Pylon* dismisses material existence far too completely to be consistent with the main thrust of Faulkner's artistic vision. Throughout his fiction, Faulkner repeatedly depicts characters who exhibit an accepting attitude toward the material world—toward dirt, odor, and excrement—positively. (One thinks, for example, of Caddy Compson's attitude toward her dirty drawers, and of the lyric description in *The Hamlet* of Ike Snopes's encounter with the cow.) To explore his imaginative relation to materialism, then, Faulkner needed to do more than depict the barnstormers' doomed efforts to transcend the physical world. He needed to find a way to rescue materialism from itself, in the sense of finding a way to reject excessive dependence on money without at the same time rejecting the life of the flesh. This he does in *The Wild Palms.*[9]

Faulkner's exploration in *The Wild Palms* of a more complex attitude toward material existence than the one he presents in *Pylon* uses a wide variety of excremental and monetary images and references. At times, these images repeat the negative association of money and excrement so prominent in *Pylon.* More often, though, Faulkner severs the connection between money and excrement and instead uses excremental and visceral imagery to signify a life-affirming acceptance of one's physical being.[10] Central to this more positive use of these sorts of images is the figurine Charlotte Rittenmeyer creates called the "Bad Smell." This figurine symbolizes an attitude Charlotte wishes to resist, both in herself and in Harry Wilbourne. As she twice tells Harry, hunger is an affair of the breast, not of the belly. In her terminology, the word "hunger" signifies desire, not appetite. In contrast to the "Bad Smell," with its "shapeless" body and "foolish disorganized face," hunger, as Charlotte visualizes it, is vivid and erotic: it looks "like a skyrocket or a roman candle or at least one of those sparkler sticks for little children that sparkle away into a live red coal that's not afraid to die" (95). But according to Charlotte, many people, including Harry, confuse hunger with fear. As she says to Harry, using the word "hungry" in its common meaning, "You've been hungry down here in your guts, so you are afraid of it" (86). Because he has lived a life of near-penury for so long, Harry may be expected to confuse emotional hunger with the fears and anxieties attending on material need. Charlotte makes the figurine to remind him—and herself—of the need to resist this confusion and to affirm the ascendancy of breast over belly, desire over fear.

Yet to formulate the significance of the figurine in this way is somewhat misleading, for the attitude Charlotte seeks to teach Harry entails more than a simple choice of breast over belly. If we ask why the figurine is called the "Bad Smell," the answer is that confusing hunger with fear paradoxically leads to an alienation from the life of the flesh. As Harry jokingly says during his and Charlotte's first meal in Wisconsin, anxiety over material need seems to have created "a gland for cowardice in [his] palate or stomach," so that instead of tasting the food he is eating, he tastes "the forty or fifty cents it represents" (104). In effect, then, anxiety over material need leads to a double repudiation, a turning aside from both breast *and* belly in the service of an illusory dream of security. Hence the name of the figurine. Charlotte calls the figurine the "Bad Smell" not because she is rejecting the life of the flesh in favor of the life of the spirit—far from it!—but because she is rejecting the souring effect of material anxiety on both dimensions of human existence.

The central action of the "Wild Palms" portion of the novel consists of Harry's struggle to assimilate and act on the lesson symbolized by the "Bad Smell." This struggle takes both psychological and social forms. Harry contemplates the first of these toward the end of "Wild Palms," as he sits awaiting word about Charlotte and reflecting on the reason (other than sickness) that people enter hospitals, which he characterizes as "carbolized vacuums . . . like wombs" (299). The reason, he says, is that people cannot bear for very long "the burden of lust and desire and pride . . . [the burden] of the old incorrigible earthly corruption" (299). So they choose to "become as embryos for a time"—but only "for a while, then to be born again, to emerge renewed, to bear the world's weight for another while as long as courage lasted" (299). The scenario Harry invokes here for the habitués of hospitals summarizes his own career in the novel, for from the moment he meets Charlotte he oscillates between affirming his lust and desire and pride and retreating into such symbolic wombs as excessive sleep, suicidal imaginings, and an obsessive concern with the state of his bank balance and the passage of time.

Accompanying this psychological struggle is a social one. In "Wild Palms," Faulkner depicts two sharply contrasting styles of life: the antiseptic, repressive, decorous style of American middle-class culture and the physically messy, emotionally open, bohemian style Harry and Charlotte attempt to follow.[11] During his and Charlotte's second residence in Chicago, Harry discovers the interconnection between his psychological anxieties and the first of these styles of life. As he tells McCord, his newspaperman friend, the relative financial security he and Charlotte achieve by his pulp writing and her work in a department store has relieved his financial fears, but at the expense of creating a related anxiety typical of American middle-class culture. "Because . . . for the first time we were solvent, knew for certain where tomorrow's food was coming from . . . ," he says, "I had become as completely thrall and slave to respectability . . . as any man by [sic] drink or opium" (133). This enthrallment is dangerous because the middle-class culture in which money and respectability are prime virtues has "got rid of love" (136). It has done so by replacing physical passion with substitute gratifications purchasable for money, so that "instead of having to save emotional currency for months and years to deserve one chance [to] spend it all for love we can now spread it thin into coppers and titillate ourselves at any newsstand" (136). Hence Harry's need to abandon his and Charlotte's comfortable existence in Chicago. By leaving for Utah, Harry seeks to extirpate from his psyche the prototypical figure of the modern age: the "husband with his Saturday pay envelope and his suburban bungalow full of electric wife-saving gadgets and his table cloth of lawn to sprinkle on Sunday morning . . . the doomed worm blind to all passion and dead to all hope and not even knowing it" (132).

Harry accompanies his insight into the cultural dimension of his anxieties with an understanding of the subversive nature of the courage required of him. As his association of courage with lust and desire and pride suggests, he does not need to exhibit courage in the sense of service to a communal ideal but in the sense of a willingness to acknowledge and act on his own desires, even when they run counter to the prevailing values of his society. In McCord's words, he needs to exhibit "the courage of [his] fornications" (101). The novel's continual testing of Harry's ability to exhibit this sort of courage reaches its first, negative climax in the botched abortion.

The need for this abortion of course arises from Charlotte's insistence that the relationship remain "all honeymoon" (83). Whatever our view of the advisability of this insistence, it should be clear that Harry's inability to perform the operation properly constitutes a failure of courage—significantly, a failure of physical courage. As his earlier operation on Billie and his willingness for Charlotte to use pills to bring about an abortion both indicate, his reluctance to operate does not arise from a concern over questions of medical ethics but from a fear—well founded, as it turns out—that he may have internalized middle-class values so completely as to be physically incapable of performing the operation.

Harry's failure of courage in the abortion sequence places him in an emotional position similar to the one occupied by the reporter at the end of *Pylon.* But here, in contrast to *Pylon,* Faulkner allows his central character to recover from the despair into which his actions have plunged him. This recovery occurs in the famous closing scene of "Wild Palms," when Harry rejects Francis Rittenmeyer's offer of a convenient means of suicide and dedicates himself to a lifetime of remembering his relationship with Charlotte. For my purposes, the most important aspect of this scene is the way in which it affirms the life of the body. At the level of thought, this affirmation takes the form, already alluded to, of a discovery of the bodily nature of memory. For his recollection of Charlotte to continue to exist, Harry realizes, memory alone—memory abstractly considered—will not suffice. This is so, he says, "*because if memory exists outside of the flesh it wont be memory because it wont know what it remembers so when she became not then half of memory became not and if I become not then all of remembering will cease to be*"; therefore, he decides, he must commit himself to "*the wheezing lungs, the troublesome guts . . . the old meat after all, no matter how old*" (324).[12]

At the level of action, Harry's newly-won commitment to the life of the flesh results in a double recovery of manual competence. Throughout the novel, Faulkner frequently uses images of hands to signify Harry's and Charlotte's access to the life of the flesh. It is appropriate, then, that Harry's failure of courage should take the form of an inability to control the trembling of his hands—most notably in the abortion sequence, but also in the beginning of the jailhouse sequence, when his hands tremble so badly that he must grasp his right wrist in his left hand before he can smoke a cigarette or drink a cup of coffee. It is highly appropriate, too, that his recovery of the will to live should enable him to perform the intricate manual act of "pinching the [cyanide] tablet in a folded cigarette paper between thumb and finger" and rubbing "the tablet carefully into powder on one of the lower bars" (323) of the cell window. Even more significant than this highly symbolic gesture, though, is Harry's second recovery of manual dexterity. Whenever Harry anticipates his breakthrough into an understanding of the physical nature of memory, he says that "it"—with the pronoun ambiguously left unreferenced—"would stand to his hand when the moment came" (324). So "it" does, for once he begins to realize that memory can only exist "in the old wheezing entrails," he starts "thinking of, remembering [Charlotte's] body, the broad thighs and the hands that liked bitching and making things"; and he thereupon discovers that "now it [does] stand to his hand, incontrovertible and plain, serene" (324).

As some early commentators observed, the language of this episode carries a very strong implication that Harry is masturbating (Jewkes; Monteiro; cf. McHaney 172–173). The line of argument I am following here supports—indeed, requires—this interpretation. Early in the novel, when Harry fantasizes about how he might spend the $300 cashier's check Francis Rittenmeyer has left with him, he says that he is engaged in "a form of masturbation" (94). This is masturbation in the sense D. H. Lawrence means when he speaks of the connection between "analysis and impotent criticism . . . and. . . . self-abuse" (23). It is masturbation used as a trope for the anxiety-ridden character of modern civilization. But Harry's final autoerotic act carries a considerably different meaning. It signifies the attitude identified by Jean-Paul Sartre in *Saint Genet,* when he says that "masturbation is the derealization of the world" and that "it elects to be a crime" (368). Halfway through the last chapter of "Wild Palms," Harry repudiates the first of the two ways in which he had been implicated in middle-class values by rejecting Francis Rittenmeyer's suggestion that he jump bail and flee with "the same three hundred dollars" (311) he had earlier fantasized about. Now he rejects the second. By incarnating his memory of Charlotte in his own flesh, he engages in an act of sexual defiance, a symbolic "derealization" of the world of middle-class respectability and an affirmation of the life of the flesh as irregular, amoral, and dangerous. And, I wish to add, he thereby completes his assimilation of the lesson symbolized by the "Bad Smell," for he performs this act while smelling the odor "of swamps and wild jasmine" brought in by "the light offshore breeze" (324)—and while smelling as well, one assumes, the underlying, ineradicable odor, indigenous to the jailhouse, of "creosote and tobacco-spit and old vomit" (308).[13]

IV

As with *Pylon,* the central action of *The Wild Palms* gains in significance when contemplated in relation to Faulkner's career. The nature of the connection between the two will begin to reveal itself if we reflect for a moment on the original title of the novel. As most readers know, Faulkner's editors rejected his preferred title, *If I Forget Thee, Jerusalem,* and substituted *The Wild Palms* instead (McHaney *William Faulkner's "The Wild Palms"* xiii; *Selected Letters* 106). When we recall the verse of Psalm 137 from which the original title was taken—"If I forget thee, O Jerusalem, let my right hand forget her cunning"—then one dimension of the superiority of the original title should become obvious. But in addition to its applicability to Harry's autoerotic reverie, the association of

Jerusalem, right hand, and cunning relates to the novel in another way, for the cunning of which the Psalmist speaks is specifically his ability to perform as an artist. Carried away into Babylon, he and his companions have "hanged [their] harps upon the willows in the midst thereof." Required by their captors to "Sing . . . one of the songs of Zion," the Psalmist asks "How shall we sing the Lord's song in a strange land?" Only if he remembers Zion in the sense of remaining loyal to her, he says, should he be permitted to play his harp and sing.

The emphasis of Psalm 137 on the relation between memory and artistic creativity gives the original title of the novel a direct biographical application. Written, as Faulkner later said, "to stave off what I thought was heartbreak" (*Selected Letters* 338), *The Wild Palms* grew directly out of the apparent termination, in late 1936, of Faulkner's affair with Meta Carpenter. For Faulkner, therefore, the Jerusalem of the original title must have symbolized his lost beloved, and the cunning of the Psalmist his ability to transform this loss into art. Without denying the pertinence of this interpretation, I wish to suggest a broader biographical symbolism for the central action of the novel. To do so, I need to make two general observations about Faulkner's understanding of his own creativity. The first is that Faulkner frequently depicts the creative process in terms reminiscent of Freud's association of creativity with the anal stage of infantile development. Whether Faulkner ever read Freud is perhaps open to question, but there can be little doubt that for Faulkner, as for Freud, human creativity begins in narcissistic self-absorption, in the infant's aimless, idle, pleasurable awareness of its own physical processes. And further, there can be little doubt that Faulkner understood his own artistic creativity to consist, in its initial stages at least, in an imaginative return to this form of infantile play.[14]

The second general observation is that Faulkner's interest in his own creativity often appears indirectly in his fiction. In

The Unmediated Vision, Geoffrey Hartman says that the ubiquitous water imagery in Wordsworth's poetry always refers to a "fundamental relation," which he formulates as "*This river: I am*" (44).[15] As with Wordsworth, so with Faulkner. By an easy transference, Faulkner extends his association of creativity with infantile narcissism to the sights, sounds, smells, and customs of the external world of his childhood. A central consequence of this extension is that Faulkner nowhere comments on social change as a dispassionate observer. When he says that he wrote *Flags in the Dust* to preserve a "world which for some reason I believe should not pass utterly out of the memory of man" (Blotner, "William Faulkner's Essay" 124), he is speaking of Oxford, Mississippi, at the turn of the century; but he is also speaking of a private, inward world whose availability to his imagination was dependent on his ability to recall the outer world of his childhood. Conversely, his sense of the threat posed to the world of his childhood by a deregionalized modern world was always personal as well, for the impending assimilation of the region of his birth by an anonymous modernity could easily be construed to be a generalized version of his own future, both as an artist and as a private individual. For Faulkner, then, the "fundamental relation" is double: both "*this South: I am*" and "*this modern world: I am not*" (cf. Minter ix–xiii, 1–23).

Viewed in these terms, the central action of "Wild Palms" can be seen to affirm an essential element of Faulkner's identity. The jangling irresolution of the conclusion of *Pylon* reflects the impasse Faulkner found himself in in 1934: disenchanted with writing for hire, yet incapable of supporting himself and his family by writing only serious fiction. But in Harry Wilbourne's abandonment of his career as a pulp writer, repudiation of middle-class values, and return to the South, we see a parabolic enactment of Faulkner's desire to resolve this impasse. Certainly the shape of Faulkner's career immediately after *The Wild Palms* supports this view, for he left Hollywood in 1937 with a definiteness he had not exhibited before, and despite economic pressures far more severe than those he had suffered in the mid-1930s, he did not seek further movie work for nearly five years.[16]

But *The Wild Palms* enacts more than a personal return to the South; it also enacts an artistic return. As Gary Harrington has shown, Harry Wilbourne is a direct fictional descendant of Quentin Compson; we may add that Charlotte Rittenmeyer, in her sensuality and physicality, is an equally direct descendant of Caddy Compson. These correspondences are important because Quentin's relation to Caddy is Faulkner's central image for his own relation to the sources of his art. In her association with childhood, dirt, and pleasure, and in her defiance of conventional morality, Caddy symbolizes the infantile narcissism out of which Faulkner's art emerged; and in his verbalism, introspection, and obsession with memory, Quentin symbolizes Faulkner's need to reconstitute this primary stratum of experience in words. When Harry commits himself to remembering Charlotte, then, he attaches the conclusion of "Wild Palms" to a central aspect of Faulkner's artistic self-understanding. And he does so, I wish to emphasize, even in the form that his rite of memory takes, for, like Quentin's imagined incest, Harry's act of masturbation expresses Faulkner's understanding of the transgressive character of his art, of its need to break through the barriers of shame and propriety and establish contact with its disorderly source.[17]

Yet in some important ways, this gesture of artistic reaffirmation expresses desire more than reality. By 1937, as Faulkner knew, the distinction between American middle-class culture and southern culture was beginning to blur. As he said in the unpublished introduction to *The Sound and the Fury* he wrote in 1933, "the South . . . is dead, killed by the Civil War. There is a thing known whimsically as the New South to be sure, but it is not the south. It is a land of Immigrants who are rebuilding the towns and cities [of the South] into replicas of towns and cities in Kansas and Iowa and Illinois" (411). Because of this blurring, returning to the South was ceasing to be an unequivocal gesture of repudiation and reaffirmation. In economic terms, taking one's stand to live and die in Dixie merely meant scrabbling for a living in a different way, as Faulkner's desperate attempts around 1940 to write money-making short stories and to seek a more lucrative publishing contract both indicate (*Selected Letters* 110–161).[18] In artistic terms, returning meant confronting the middle-class materialism depicted in *The Wild Palms* on more intimate and more troubling grounds. Understandably, then, in his next two novels Faulkner turns to southern versions of the monetary theme of *Pylon* and *The Wild Palms*: in *The Hamlet* to a depiction of the economic transformation of southern society, and in *Go Down, Moses* to a depiction of Ike McCaslin's agonized attempt—so similar and yet so different from Harry Wilbourne's—to reject his cultural heritage.

In another way, too, *The Wild Palms* looks somewhat uneasily toward the future. Harry Wilbourne affirms memory, desire, and the life of the flesh; but to do so, he must overcome his own deep inclination to abide by the behavioral norms of his society. His struggle over this issue reflects an emerging struggle within Faulkner himself, between the artistic self-understanding described above and a desire to make his art more explicitly social and ethical in its orientation—a desire to become, as he said in a letter written in 1942, "articulate in the national voice" (*Selected Letters* 166). This socializing and ethicalizing impulse never completely dominates Faulkner's understanding of himself as an artist; but to the extent it does, it inhibits his access to the deepest sources of his creativity. These observations allow me to add a final element to my interpretation of the novel's biographical symbolism. Harry Wilbourne's imprisonment in the last chapter of "Wild Palms" marks the first time in his fiction that Faulkner incarcerates a self-representational character. It will not be the last. Throughout his later fiction—in *Requiem for a Nun* and *A Fable,* as we have already seen, but also in *Go*

Down, Moses, Intruder in the Dust, and *The Mansion*—Faulkner places characters who function as authorial surrogates in prisons and prison-like settings. On all these occasions, although with varying degrees of explicitness, he uses these settings to explore the apparent slackening of his creative power. In Harry Wilbourne's imprisonment, then, we see the first foreshadowing of a central concern of the second half of Faulkner's career. Harry Wilbourne returns to the South and to the irregular life of the flesh, and in terms of Faulkner's art, this is good. But we should not forget the future Faulkner has reserved for Harry: it consists of fifty years of hard labor in the state of Mississippi.

THREE

The Dream of Freedom

The search for resemblances between Faulkner and his fictional characters often reveals more about the predispositions of those who engage in it than it does about either Faulkner or his creations. But in the case of *Go Down, Moses,* one such correspondence seems almost to force itself on our attention. Like Faulkner at the time he was writing the novel, Roth Edmonds is a man in his early forties. He lives on a plantation that bears approximately the same geographical relation to the fictional Jefferson as does Greenfield Farm—purchased by Faulkner in 1938—to the town of Oxford. By all accounts, his relations with Lucas Beauchamp and his wife Molly resemble, in tone if not in detail, those that Faulkner had with Ned Barnett, a long-time family servant, and Caroline Barr, the "Mammy" of the novel's dedication. Most of all, though, Roth resembles his creator in his dominant emotional state: like Faulkner in the early 1940s, Roth is a man driven almost to distraction by the demands, both social and economic, being made on him by the people among whom he lives.[1]

Characters who are harassed by either social or economic obligations or both of course appear frequently in Faulkner's fiction. One thinks, for example, of the sculptor Gordon in *Mosquitoes,* of Jason Compson in *The Sound and the Fury,* and (as we have just seen) of the barnstormers in *Pylon* and Harry Wilbourne in *The Wild Palms.* There are particular reasons, however, why a character of this sort should figure prominently in *Go Down, Moses.* As Joseph Blotner's *Faulkner: A Bi-*

ography and Faulkner's letters both make clear, the two years or so prior to the publication of the novel constituted the most intense period of economic uncertainty that Faulkner ever endured. Also, for the first time in his career, Faulkner began to express dismay over the nature and extent of his social obligations, complaining that they were interfering with his ability to write. These circumstances encouraged Faulkner to view the fundamental antinomy of his artistic identity—the opposition between the creative self and the South on the one hand and the modern world on the other—in a new way, as an opposition between the creative self and all forms of social existence. In *Go Down, Moses,* Faulkner explores this way of understanding his artistic identity, creating in the process an enduring meditation on the theme of freedom and a foreboding anticipation of the shape of his artistic future.

I

The story of Faulkner's economic and creative circumstances in the early 1940s makes melancholy reading. Faulkner first wrote several of the stories from which *Go Down, Moses* was formed as part of a generally unsuccessful attempt to earn enough money from the slick magazines to free himself for work on more serious fiction. The inception of his work on the novel itself was delayed first by a desperate attempt to see if changing publishers might free him from the need to write magazine stories, and, when this failed, by further work on such stories. After his work on the novel actually did begin, he was forced to interrupt it at least twice, once to write a simplified version of "The Bear" for submission to *The Saturday Evening Post,* and a second time to work on a new story line for a movie script. Throughout this period, he frequently had to draw advances from his publisher. On one occasion he had to borrow money from Harold Ober, his agent, and on another he had to accept Ober's generosity in foregoing the commission on a story that Faulkner, in his anxiety for a quick sale, had submitted directly to a magazine. Three months after the novel appeared, he wrote Bennett Cerf, saying "I have 60c in my pocket, and that is literally all" (*Selected Letters* 154). In a letter to Ober written at the same time, he said that he owed "the grocer $600.00," had "no fuel for the winter yet," (154) and was looking for a way to get to California, where he hoped to pick up some work writing for the movies.[2]

Taken all in all, then, it is scarcely surprising that in the early 1940s Faulkner felt himself to be "not quite a boat's length ahead of the sheriff," or that he occasionally began "to seethe and rage. . . . and . . . waste time when [he] might and should [have been] writing" (*Selected Letters* 149, 123). But what interpretation should we place on the circumstances I have just described? In one regard, to be sure, their significance is clear enough: it lies in what they tell us about our culture. For Blotner, for Malcolm Cowley before him, and for many other readers as well, Faulkner's situation in the early 1940s is a damning example of the philistinism inherent in America's treatment of its greatest literary artist during the middle years of his career. Its salient feature is its "ironic juxtaposition of mastery and unpaid bills" (Blotner, *Faulkner: A Biography* 1032), and its source, as Cowley says (quoting Henry James), is "a want in the public taste" (*Portable Faulkner* x).[3]

This view has much to recommend it. One cannot come away from Blotner's somber account of Faulkner's movement into bondage to Warner Brothers without a sense of outrage that it ever had to happen. Yet both Faulkner's letters and Blotner's biography suggest that this interpretation, while not inaccurate, is radically incomplete. It is clear that during this time Faulkner was chronically and desperately in need of money. But his impecuniousness needs to be viewed in relation not only to the general cultural indifference to his art but to the really quite extraordinary level of social and material obligation he had imposed upon himself. As he said in a letter to Robert Haas, although undoubtedly with some exaggeration, he had come to be "the sole, principal and partial support—food, shelter, heat, clothes, medicine, kotex, school fees, toilet paper, and picture shows—of [his] mother, an inept brother and his wife and two sons, another brother's widow and child, a wife of [his] own and two step children, [and his] own child" (Blotner, *Faulkner: A Biography* 1044; cf. *Selected Letters* 122). Along with the expenses entailed by these social relationships, he was responsible for the mortgages, taxes, and upkeep on a 320-acre farm and on his own homestead, which by this time amounted to "35 acres of wooded parkland inside [the] Oxford corporate limits" (*Selected Letters* 127). In a word, he was land and relative-poor.[4]

The question that arises here is whether he had to be. To what extent, that is, were the responsibilities that made Faulkner so needful of money in the early 1940s imposed from without and to what extent were they the result of his own choices? In the area of his social obligations, the answer to these questions is mixed. The need to support himself and his own immediate family was, of course, not seriously open to question. And in the instance of his brother Dean's widow and child, where a choice would seem to have been available, Faulkner's sense of guilt over the manner of his brother's death may have made it necessary for him to contribute to their support.[5] But where choices clearly did exist, as in his continued (and apparently unaided) maintenance of a separate household for his mother, or his hiring of his brother John to manage Greenfield Farm, Faulkner's impulse seems consistently to have been to increase his social responsibilities rather than to lessen them. And in the matter of the purchase of land, the situation is quite unambiguous. Throughout the 1930s, Faulkner strove tenaciously to increase his holdings in real property, even at the risk of occasionally over-extending his financial resources. In 1931, less than a year after the initial down payment on the house that was to become Rowan Oak, Faulkner was forced to defer payments on his mortgage for a few months. Yet in 1933, after an initial visit to Hollywood that was occasioned in part by his need to meet his mortgage obligations, he extended his indebtedness through the purchase of three lots adjoining his property. And in 1938, when faced with a $19,000 windfall resulting from the sale of the film rights to *The Unvanquished,* he again responded characteristically, using the bulk of the money (plus a $2000 loan) to purchase and stock Greenfield Farm, and part of the remainder to make a down payment toward the purchase of Bailey's Woods, the final segment of his Oxford holdings (Blotner, *Faulkner: A Biography* 689, 803, 983–987).

In sum, Faulkner helped create the difficulties he faced by his willingness to take on responsibilities within his family and by his eagerness to acquire property. This conclusion may seem a negative judgment on Faulkner's ability to manage his resources—a way of saying that had he been less regardful of the needs of his relatives or less desirous of living in a large house, then his impoverishment at the time he was writing *Go Down, Moses* would have been less acute. But the art of Faulkner's necessities was strange. Rather than leading us to doubt his managerial abilities (which were actually rather good), Faulkner's financial and social conduct during the 1930s should instead suggest the depth of the emotional need to which it was a response. Viewed in retrospect, Faulkner's actions display an internal coherence. Although he was by nature a financially cautious man, he was audacious in his purchases during this period (and in his acceptance of responsibility) because he was actualizing a deeply cherished vision of his proper role in the world. He was willing to run the risk of impoverishment, in cash terms at least, in order to become something he evidently very deeply needed to be: a paterfamilias, the owner of a mansion, the master of a plantation.

Rowan Oak, Greenfield Farm, and their attendant responsibilities, then, were elements in a fiction, insofar as Faulkner was using them as a way of expressing his vision of himself in relation to the world. Now it is true that all of our expenditures of money and energy beyond the subsistence level have this expressive quality; how we spend our substance is a statement about who we are or who we wish to be. But Faulkner's use of this means of self-expression has greater than usual significance because of the intricate and revealing relation it bears to his art. What began simply as a form of self-expression parallel to his art ultimately came into conflict with it. By the early 1940s, Faulkner's ownership of property and assumption of familial responsibilities had helped to heighten a fundamental ambivalence in his conception of himself as an artist and had begun to work a noticeable alteration in the nature of his fiction.

The most apparent point of contact between Faulkner's art and the shape he attempted to give to his life in Oxford is that both are acts of memorialization. Just as Faulkner's Yoknapatawpha fiction arose in large measure out of his sense of nostalgia, so also did his style of life. As Blotner's biography and such other works as John Faulkner's *My Brother Bill* and Malcolm Franklin's *Bitterweeds* indicate, life at both Rowan Oak and Greenfield Farm was marked by willfully imposed elements of anachronism. Faulkner refused, for example, to allow a radio in Rowan Oak until his daughter was a teenager.[6] At his insistence, the main activity at Greenfield Farm was the breeding and sale of mules, a choice which, although mules were not entirely outmoded in the south in 1940, was apparently made more for symbolic reasons than for economic ones (John Faulkner 159). And although he fulminated against the obligations imposed upon him by his having "inherited [his] father's . . . dependents, white and black" (*Selected Letters* 122), he was careful to maintain an old-fashioned set of familial and master-servant relationships at both his house and his farm.

Like his art, then, the style of life Faulkner developed for himself constituted a memorialization of passing values. It also resembled his art in being an implicit criticism of the modern world for having abandoned those values. It combined, although necessarily in muted form, the twin motives

Faulkner attributed to the southern artist in his 1933 introduction to *The Sound and the Fury:* "to draw a savage indictment of the contemporary scene" and "to escape from it into a makebelieve region of swords and magnolias and mockingbirds" (412). Yet in creating this parallel between his life and his art, Faulkner involved himself—perhaps inevitably—in an ironic confusion of means and ends. To raise mules on his farm, he had to buy a tractor (John Faulkner 159–160). The farm itself, which symbolized an agrarian order whose continued existence seemed threatened by the "W.P.A. and XYZ" of governmental agencies, required for its purchase a loan from such an agency.[7] On a larger scale, more familiar versions of the same irony occurred. In order to live at Rowan Oak, Faulkner had to work periodically in Hollywood, that citadel of modernity. When this expedient failed (or was resisted), he had to "boil the pot" by writing magazine stories. And in both instances, he had to steal time from his primary medium of self-expression to feed his secondary one.

In a subtler way as well, the parallel between Faulkner's life and his art reveals an underlying conflict. When viewed from outside—from Hollywood, say—the South could appear to be an adequate objective correlative for the deepest and most inward dimension of Faulkner's art. But experiencing the South from inside, as it actually existed in the 1930s and 1940s, necessarily revealed the inadequacy of the equation "*this South: I am.*" Faulkner anticipates this observation in the version of the *Sound and the Fury* introduction cited above, when, after talking about the emergence of the New South, he says, "it is himself that the Southerner is writing about, not about his environment: who has, figuratively speaking, taken the artist in him in one hand and his milieu in the other and thrust the one into the other like a clawing and spitting cat into a croker sack" (412). Revealed in this comment is Faulkner's understanding that at some level his art was always an alternative to life in the South—and to all forms of social existence—rather than an extension or a reflection of it. As he says, the private significance of his art lay in "the emotion definite and physical and yet nebulous to describe which the writing of Benjy's section of *The Sound and the Fury* gave me—that ecstasy, that eager and joyous faith and anticipation of surprise which the yet unmarred sheets beneath my hand held inviolate and unfailing" (414). And as he also says, this sense of ecstatic union with the process of writing depended on a deliberate act of psychic withdrawal; only when it seemed that "a door had clapped silently and forever to" between him and all questions of publishers or of audiences was he able to say, "Now I can write. Now I can just write" (412–413).

In effect, then, we have three terms: Faulkner's artistic identity; his society as it happened to exist; and his attempt to establish a style of life mediating between the two. This attempt could not express the full range of Faulkner's understanding of himself as an artist. It was capable of incorporating both his nostalgia and his criticism of the contemporary world, but by its nature it could not express the private center of his art, for this constituted itself in a radical *ir*responsibility, in a dream of imaginative self-fulfillment beyond all social or material constraint. By the early 1940s, Faulkner himself had begun to reach this conclusion. In the letter to Robert Haas in which he listed his social responsibilities, he characterized himself as "an artist, a sincere one and of the first class, who should be free even of his own economic responsibilities and with no moral conscience at all" (*Selected Letters* 122). In stating this desire for freedom from obligation, Faulkner expressed a wish he returned to with increasing frequency as his career advanced. In a letter to Malcolm Cowley written in 1946, for example, he spoke of how he had "become the slave of [a] vast and growing mass of inanimate junk . . . not one piece of which" he really wanted (*Selected Letters* 245). And in essays, interviews, and class conferences, he returned repeatedly to the notion that his true identity was as "a tramp, a harmless possessionless vagabond" (*Essays* 21), and he suggested, only half jokingly, that he had chosen writing as his profession because it seemed to promise him more freedom from responsibility than did any other form of livelihood.[8]

The form Faulkner's life had taken by the early 1940s thus can be seen to have been inimical to his art not only in the demands it placed on his time and energy but in the way it contradicted an important aspect of his artistic identity. There remains yet a further level of complication. For Faulkner, the most distressing aspect of the social and financial harassment he was undergoing was its ability to interfere with his work. In his words, he was "so busy borrowing money from Random House" that he didn't "even have time to write" (*Selected Letters* 125). In a limited sense, this was undoubtedly true: the contemplated change of publishers, for example, entailed several lengthy and carefully thought-out letters, as well as a time-consuming trip to New York. But with the benefit of hindsight, we can see that the ultimate cause of Faulkner's difficulty in writing (the first he ever complained of, as Blotner notes) was nothing less than the diminution in his creative drive that began in the early 1940s. Although Faulkner was reluctant to admit it, the great outpouring of the 1930s was ceasing, to return only intermittently during the rest of his career. With this change came a problem in how he was to use his time. Where before his difficulty had been to find ways to keep up with his imagination, it now was to find ways to wait for it. At some unconscious level, then, Faulkner may have been seeking out and even welcoming the disruptive complications his life was displaying. Like his later restless travel and his assumption of the role of lecturer and public man, his social and financial obligations served a purpose in his life. They created a kind of busywork that could simultaneously fill the void caused by his failure to write and be used as an excuse for it.

II

But he did write *Go Down, Moses*. Although premonitions of the six years of silence that followed the publication of this novel crop up during the time of its composition, Faulkner was able to turn them to fictional account. As had other artists before him, he used the threatened departure of the visionary gleam as a subject for its further efflorescence. He did the same with the whole range of social and economic difficulties he was undergoing at the time he was writing the novel. He occasionally made direct use of these experiences, transferring a detail from his daily life or a phrase from one of his letters into the text of the novel. More frequently, he transformed them, converting the emerging tension between his artistic and social identities into a searching fictional reflection on the themes of freedom and bondage, individuality and community, self-realization and self-defeat.

How this process works can be seen in "The Fire and the Hearth, the novella-length second section of *Go Down, Moses.* Faulkner's most direct self-reference in the whole of the novel occurs here, in the figure of Roth Edmonds. In Roth, we see a humorous depiction of the stresses Faulkner was undergoing. Like his creator, Roth feels alternating worry and outrage over the demands being made on him, even though, because he is parentless and a bachelor, they originate not with relatives but with the tenants on his plantation. Like Faulkner, too, he preserves as many elements as possible of a past order. He tries "even with the changed times" to run the plantation "as his father and grandfather and great-grandfather had done before him," overseeing the work from horseback, stopping ritualistically once a month to visit with Molly Beauchamp, and in general showing a paternal regard for the well-being of all of his tenants (116). And because it appears to him that his only reward for his concern is the "accumulation of floutings and outrages" (104) that Lucas Beauchamp visits on him, he falls at times—once again like Faulkner—into "a kind of vindictive exultation" (85) over the extent to which he is being mistreated.

Accompanying this parallel is a somewhat less apparent one between Faulkner and Lucas Beauchamp. Lucas stands in a complex expressive relation to his creator. On the one hand, he functions as the comic villain in a Faulknerian fantasy of inverse social oppression. As he takes repeated advantage of Roth, he comes to symbolize the "long and unbroken course of outrageous trouble and conflict" (116) that both Roth's and Faulkner's attempts to preserve a traditional social order entailed for them. On the other hand, Lucas is a direct authorial surrogate, in that he embodies Faulkner's dream of an existence free from social and material constraint. At the outset of "The Fire and the Hearth," Lucas is in the same situation with respect to his wife and daughter as Roth is in later with regard to him. Because of his wife's age and his daughter's involvement with George Wilkins, "the two people from whom he might reasonably and logically have not only expected but demanded help" are not only "completely interdict[ed]" (34) to him but are, in the person of his daughter at least, an actual threat to his future well-being. In this instance, Lucas shares one of Roth's resemblances to Faulkner, for like Roth he experiences his social existence as a set of burdens and impediments. But unlike Roth, Lucas never threatens to be overwhelmed by the demands that his relationships make on him. Significantly, he is described as being free from both "material shackles" and "moral ones" (105). He has "more money in the bank . . . than he will ever spend" (33), and he possesses "the use and benefit of the land" on which he lives "with none of the responsibilities" (44). As Roth comes to realize, Lucas is largely impervious to emotional ties as well, for he is willing to push both his marriage and his relationship with Roth to the edge of destruction before conceding his need for either of them.

The notion that Lucas embodies a Faulknerian dream of freedom from constraint takes on added interest because of his race. A central question to be raised about *Go Down, Moses* is why, at this point in his career, Faulkner should have turned his attention to a black character of Lucas's sort. In one regard, the answer to this question is immediately apparent.

The Lucas Beauchamp of *Go Down, Moses* is a stage in the examination of southern black life that begins in *Soldiers' Pay* and *Flags in the Dust,* develops through *The Sound and the Fury* and *Absalom, Absalom!*, and culminates in *Intruder in the Dust,* in Faulkner's second depiction of Lucas. But this pattern of development can obscure our understanding of Lucas's role in *Go Down, Moses* if it leads us to view him exclusively in representational terms or to assimilate his appearance in the novel to the rather more ideologically freighted one he makes in *Intruder in the Dust.* If we instead look at Lucas in relation to Faulkner's expressive needs at the time he was writing *Go Down, Moses*, then one fact immediately stands out: with Lucas, Faulkner comes closer than at any other point in his career to ceding narratorial authority to a black character.[9]

This fact suggests that in developing Lucas as an embodiment of his fantasy of freedom Faulkner also forged a link between Lucas and his conception of himself as an artist. Stated more generally, it suggests the existence in Faulkner's mind of a sequence of associations that ran *artist : freedom from responsibility : Negro.* Given the ubiquity in American culture of images of the artist as a bohemian and of the Negro as a carefree Sambo, we might reasonably expect Faulkner to have framed this sequence of associations even if we had no evidence that he ever actually did so. But as John T. Irwin suggests, we can in fact sense its presence at a number of points in Faulkner's fiction. In *Mosquitoes*, Faulkner jokingly describes himself as "a liar by profession" and "a little kind of black man," although not "a nigger" (144–145). In *Absalom, Absalom!*, he creates a complex variation on the sequence when he links Quentin Compson's interest in Charles Bon's blackness to Quentin's need to narrate the Sutpen story and to his obsession with the "dark half" of his own personality (Irwin, *Doubling and Incest* 36–37, 167–168). And it is clear that the sequence was on Faulkner's mind at the time he was writing *Go Down, Moses*, for in the letter to Robert Haas already cited he concludes his complaint about the incongruity of an artist such as himself having to bear financial responsibility by saying that he needs to learn "some East Indian process to attain to the nigger attitude about debt" (*Selected Letters* 123).

To see the full pertinence of this link between Lucas and Faulkner's conception of himself as an artist, we need to return for a moment to the unpublished introduction to *The Sound and the Fury*. In both versions of the introduction, Faulkner describes his career subsequent to 1929 as a series of failed attempts to recapture the "ecstasy" he experienced in writing the novel; he concludes, in the language of the longer version, that the ecstasy "will not return" and that his future emotional response to the act of writing will have to consist only of "cold satisfaction in work well and arduously done" (414–415). This scenario enacts a variation on the understanding of the creative process explored in Chapter Two. In its self-communing, self-delighting quality, the ecstasy Faulkner associates with the writing of *The Sound and the Fury* resembles the infantile narcissism out of which he believed his creativity to arise; while his description of his career subsequent to 1929 exemplifies his view of writing as a doomed attempt to recapture this primal experience in words. This way of understanding his career (and his creativity) easily could be restated as a struggle between self and society. By a simple transference of terms, Faulkner could view his journey into social existence—both the lifelong one originating in infancy and the adult one originating in marriage and home ownership—as the means by which his experience of ecstasy had been betrayed.[10]

An underlying sense that social existence is a form of self-betrayal gives "The Fire and the Hearth" much of its complexity and interest. The overt action of the narrative clearly is ameliorative, dealing with the reestablishment of Lucas's communal ties after his threatened abandonment of them. This action joins with the characterization of Roth to express—and, in a sense, to attempt to justify—the social and financial complications Faulkner experienced in the early 1940s. Working against this dominant movement of the story, though, is Faulkner's covert admiration for Lucas's intransigence. Although Faulkner evokes sympathy for Roth's beleaguered effort to preserve the plantation social order, the primary impression he creates of Roth is of someone who is a "lesser man" (59) than Lucas because he is more fully socialized. Roth has learned all the social virtues—"to be gentle with his inferiors, honorable with his equals, generous to the weak and considerate of the aged, courteous, truthful and brave to all" (117)—but the effect of these has been to create in him, in contrast to Lucas's "composed" and "ruthless" (108) self-regard, a debilitating sort of selflessness. Throughout the narrative, Lucas is characterized by a series of adjectives that emphasize his separate, self-contained, self-sufficient quality. He is "inscrutable," "intact," "indifferent," "impervious," "impassive," "impenetrable." But Roth, in a contrast that gains significance when viewed in relation to the attitudes toward sound and silence detailed in Chapter One, is so fully socialized as not even to be able to remain silent for long. He enters the narrative talking, and he soon begins "to roar," to speak "violently," to "curse," to speak in "a shaking voice," to speak in a "hoarse strangled voice," "to roar again." Like a comic version of Horace Benbow or Gavin Stevens, Roth reveals by his volubility his lack of an independent identity.

Most of all, though, Roth is a lesser man than Lucas because of the way he responds to the past—specifically to the idea of ancestry. Roth broaches this subject, in an otherwise puzzlingly inconsequent passage, when he recalls "that moment when, enveloped and surrounded still by the warmth and confidence [of childhood], . . . the child realizes with both grief and outrage that the parent antedates it" (115). Although Roth recalls an initial reaction of "grief and outrage" here, he more typically responds to his awareness of his belatedness by acknowledging the superiority of the past to the present and of his ancestors to himself. Hence his many little acts of homage and remembrance: the candy once a month for Molly; the continued payment of "fifty dollars a month" (107) to Isaac McCaslin; the acknowledgment of the validity of Lucas's inheritance of his cabin and land "without recourse for life" (116). But Lucas, we know, is "ancestryless"—or, in the fuller phrasing provided by Isaac McCaslin in "The Bear," he is "by himself composed, himself selfprogenitive and nominate, by himself ancestored" (281). Alone among the characters in *Go Down, Moses,* Lucas has abrogated the power of succession and overcome the tyranny of time. How he has done this (other than by accepting his legacy from L. Q. C. McCaslin and changing his name from "Lucius" to "Lucas") is not clear. But the point at issue is not the representational clarity of "The Fire and the Hearth" but its expressive power. Regardless of how Lucas achieves his victory over time, we can see in it a version of Faulkner's wish that his art could itself achieve such a victory. And in the sequence of associations I have examined here, we can see the connection Faulkner drew between this wish and his sense that an opposition necessarily exists between the artist and society.

III

In opposing the artist to society under the figure of the opposition between Lucas and Roth, Faulkner opposed himself to himself. Here we see an inherent limitation in his use of "The Fire and the Hearth" as an expressive instrument. By its nature, the action of "The Fire and the Hearth" required that Faulkner translate the internal relation between his artistic and social identities into an external opposition between characters; the effect of this translation was to schematize the relation and to simplify some of its complexities. To overcome this limitation, Faulkner needed to do two things. He needed to depict his artistic and his social self-definitions as residing inside a single character, and he needed to devise an action in which these self-definitions were placed not only in external but also in internal conflict. He needed, in short, to invent Isaac McCaslin and to write "The Bear."[11]

When viewed in broad outline, the expressive structure of "The Bear" may appear to repeat that of "The Fire and the Hearth." Again we have a sympathetic character—this time McCaslin Edmonds, Roth's grandfather—who has "one foot straddled into a farm and the other foot straddled into a bank" (250). And in Isaac McCaslin we have a character who stands in the same sort of attitudinal opposition to McCaslin Edmonds as Lucas does to Roth. Here too, we see Faulkner expressing his dream of freedom from constraint, for when Ike journeys into the wilderness, he joins a group of beings who are defined primarily in terms of their freedom from relation: Lion, who "dont care about nothing or nobody" (220); Sam Fathers, "childless, kinless, peopleless" (246); and "the old male bear itself, so long unwifed and childless as to have become its own ungendered progenitor" (210). But the two works differ in the form the dream of freedom takes. To the extent that Lucas's way of freeing himself from social dependency is represented in "The Fire and the Hearth," it consists of the single, self-contained symbolic gesture of changing his name. Ike's relation to the dream of freedom is more complex, for his journey into the wilderness is not simply a gesture but a continuing action.

This difference makes Ike a more supple expressive instrument than Lucas. Lucas's "selfprogenitive" gesture has a sort of continuous existence parallel to his being in time but independent of it. As a result, although he can embody the union of the self with the self that is the ultimate source (and goal) of Faulkner's art, he cannot embody the condition of authorship itself, for this arises, in John T. Irwin's phrase, from "a sense of the loss of the original virgin space" (*Doubling and Incest* 170). Ike, by contrast, can express both. In his rebirth in the wilderness he undergoes an experience equivalent in meaning to Lucas's gesture of self-creation: by coming into union with the wilderness, he comes (at least in his view) into union with his own authentic self. But this rebirth is subject, in a way Lucas's gesture is not, to what Faulkner elsewhere calls "the dark, harsh flowing of time" ("An Introduction to *The Sound and the Fury*" 413). Even at the age of ten, Ike "divines" that the wilderness is "doomed" (193). He is willing to engage in the hunt for the bear because he realizes, as Sam Fathers says, that "somebody is going to [kill it], some day" (212). And when Old Ben's death and the subsequent closing of the hunting camp actually do occur, Ike becomes eligible to function as a kind of author, a role he in fact assumes in the fourth section of "The Bear," when he translates his experience in the wilderness into a fiction of the fall of the American Eden and then uses this fiction to explain and justify his decision to relinquish his inheritance.

"The Bear" thus becomes a parable of the career of the artist as Faulkner understood it: an original sense of ecstasy, followed by a falling away, followed by an attempt to recapture the original ecstasy in words. As stated here, this pattern may appear capable of being repeated indefinitely without variation. But it is itself subject to the flow of time. In "The Bear," that is, Faulkner could not simply reenact the understanding of his art he first stated in the unpublished introduction to *The Sound and the Fury*. He had to adjust it—even if unconsciously—to the changes that were taking place in his situation as an artist. Specifically, he had to find a way of responding to the two fears he began to experience in the early 1940s: the fear that his artistic subject matter was disappearing and the fear that his creative drive was beginning to diminish.

The adjustment Faulkner makes consists essentially of narrowing the gap between the artist and society. It manifests itself in his choice of Ike McCaslin as authorial surrogate and in the nature of the fiction he assigns to Ike. As studies of the genesis of *Go Down, Moses* show, in the short stories out of which "The Bear" was formed, Ike McCaslin's role is occupied by Quentin Compson.[12] When we connect this fact with the interpretation of Harry Wilbourne's fictional ancestry advanced in Chapter Two, we arrive at a three-stage genealogy that runs from Quentin Compson to Harry Wilbourne to Isaac McCaslin. If we ask how the second and third characters in this line of descent differ from the first, a simple but important answer is that they survive. In a large sense, all of Faulkner's *artistes manqués* after *The Sound and the Fury* are attempts to allow Quentin Compson to survive, insofar as they are attempts to combine Faulkner's self-delighting understanding of his artistic identity with his understanding of himself as a social and ethical being. In *The Wild Palms,* this attempt takes the form of enclosing Harry's act of self-pleasuring inside the social gesture of grieving for Charlotte. In "The Bear," it takes the form of enclosing Ike's continuing allegiance to the wilderness—to ecstatic selfhood—inside his rejection of slavery and property ownership.[13]

Similar considerations apply to the fiction Ike creates in the fourth section of "The Bear." It is a truism to say that Faulkner's novels of the late 1920s and 1930s interrogate received structures of meaning. Time and again in the fiction of this period, repositories of belief central to our culture—religion, nature, race, history, memory, gender—are deconstructed, in the sense that their promise of affording us an absolute or transcendental ground for the establishment of meaning and value is called into question. But the fiction Ike McCaslin creates attempts to rehabilitate some of these concepts. In imagining the wilderness as "bigger and older than any recorded document" (191), for example, Ike resurrects the romantic view of nature as external to culture and history—a view which, as we saw in Chapter One, Quentin Compson discovers to be invalid. In much the same way, Ike attempts to rehabilitate the idea of religion. In a review of *The Old Man and the Sea* written shortly after the novel appeared, Faulkner congratulated Hemingway on having "discovered God" (*Essays* 193). In Hemingway's earlier fiction, he said, Hemingway's "men and women had made themselves, shaped themselves out of their own clay" (193). In this comment, Faulkner could as well have been speaking of Quentin Compson, Darl Bundren or, as we have seen, Lucas Beauchamp. But when Ike introduces "this Arbiter, this Architect, this Umpire" (258) into the fiction he creates and then proceeds to devise a plot based on a providential view of history, he signals Faulkner's desire to relinquish his earlier skepticism in favor of more conventional religious beliefs.[14]

This desire is part of a larger modification that was taking place in Faulkner's relation to society. As he sensed the decline in his creative drive, Faulkner evidently felt the need for a more complete rapprochement with society than any he had previously undergone. How this need was to affect his subsequent career can be glimpsed in "Delta Autumn" and "Go Down, Moses," the last two sections of *Go Down, Moses*. In a letter to Malcolm Cowley in which he protested against a proposed *Life* magazine article on his life and works, Faulkner said that it was his "ambition to be, as a private individual, abolished and voided from history, leaving it markless, no refuse save the printed books" (*Selected Letters* 285). He said that he wanted his "obit and epitaph too" to be "he made the books and he died" (285). Here we have the clearest expression in the whole of Faulkner's career of his desire that his life be coterminous with his art. When "Delta Autumn" is considered in expressive terms, it reveals traces of this same desire. Much of the power of the section, in fact, lies in the impression it gives of being a personal valediction, so that when Ike dreams of "the two spans" of his life and of the wilderness "running out together" (354), we sense that Faulkner has in mind the end not only of an epoch in our civilization but of a period in his own artistic history—perhaps even of the entirety of that history.[15]

But Faulkner's life and art did not end together. Faulkner lived not only past the period of his daemonic ecstasy but also past the time of his cold satisfaction in the recollection of it. And in using Gavin Stevens as an authorial surrogate in such later novels as *Intruder in the Dust*, *The Town*, and *The Mansion*, he created a distinctive addition to the line of descent running from Quentin Compson to Isaac McCaslin, one through which he could explore and perhaps affirm the shared values of his culture. Yet Faulkner's commitment to Stevens as an authorial surrogate is never unequivocal, and such attractions as the late novels display reside largely in the ways the desire for rapprochement is evaded, resisted, and denied. It is perhaps appropriate, then, that *Go Down, Moses* does not end—as it could have—with Ike's dream of himself and the wilderness "running out together" but instead concludes with the first full-scale appearance of Stevens in the Faulknerian oeuvre. And it is surely appropriate that Stevens's attempt in "Go Down, Moses" to create a fiction in the service of the prevailing social order should cost him time and money and leave him feeling harassed.

FOUR

The Uses of the Imagination

For both thematic and formal reasons, *Requiem for a Nun* poses severe problems for interpretation. Thematically, the novel resists interpretation because of the odd character of its central action. To suggest, as Faulkner apparently does, that Nancy Mannigoe can only preserve Temple Drake's marriage by murdering her youngest child commits an outrage, in Michael Millgate's words, "not simply upon our moral sensibilities but on our credulity" (223). Yet to attempt to overcome this outrage by interpreting Nancy as a murderess rather than as a martyr, as Noel Polk has done, would seem to reverse the difficulty without resolving it.[1] When approached in formal terms, the novel presents an equally knotty problem, in that the interconnections between the dramatic and narrative sections are so few in number and so general in character as to prevent us from answering satisfactorily the question of the novel's coherence. After we have noted these interconnections, we are left agreeing with Cleanth Brooks, when he says that the structure of *Requiem for a Nun* "constitutes the most daring but perhaps the least successful solution of the structural problems attempted by Faulkner in any of his novels" (*William Faulkner: The Yoknapatawpha Country* 140).

Before we accede entirely to this judgment, though, we ought to consider the possibility that it may arise more from our way of reading than from the novel itself. Interpretations of *Requiem for a Nun* created under the aegis of New Criticism exhibit New Criticism's strengths, but also its limitations. They explore quite well those features of the novel that are consistent with a view of it as an autonomous formal artifact; but they are almost entirely silent about the novel's expressive dimension.[2] Yet as Joseph Blotner's *Faulkner: A Biography,* David Minter's *William Faulkner: His Life and Work,* and Judith Bryant Wittenberg's *Faulkner: The Transfiguration of Biography* have argued, and as this book confirms, it is always dangerous to ignore the expressive element in Faulkner's art. His own disclaimers to the contrary, Faulkner is one of the most intensely personal of all major American writers, not in the sense that his novels provide a direct transcription of the events of his life, which they rarely do, but in the sense that his universal, public meanings always have at their core a meditation on some aspect of his psychic life or of his relation with the world.

If we read *Requiem for a Nun* with the intention of allowing its personal meanings to emerge, then a number of features of the novel immediately demand our attention, all of which have to do with Faulkner's understanding of himself as an artist. That this matter should have been of concern at the time of the writing of *Requiem for a Nun* will scarcely surprise us if we recall the circumstances out of which the novel arose. Shortly before writing the novel, Faulkner underwent the long period of artistic silence extending from the completion of *Go Down, Moses* in late 1941 to the writing of *Intruder in the Dust* in 1948. The narrative and dramatic sections of *Requiem for a Nun* enact, in different but related ways, Faulkner's attempt to work through the implications of this period of creative blockage.[3] In both parts of the novel, Faulkner places extraordinary emphasis on acts of reading and writing; in both, he explores the relation between imagination and time; in both, he depicts a change, or an attempted change, from one way of understanding and using the imagination to another. By doing so, he creates a moving elegy to the disappearance of his earlier artistic self-understanding and of the pre-modern South, and he opens the way for his reuse of his Yoknapatawpha subject matter in his subsequent novels.

I

In the dramatic sections of *Requiem for a Nun*, Faulkner's act of artistic self-scrutiny takes the form of a struggle between two views of the function of the imagination, one of which is embodied in Temple Drake, the other in Gavin Stevens. The nature of the view embodied in Temple will become apparent if we reflect for a moment on the relation between the letters she wrote in the Manuel Street bordello and her sexual experiences with Alabama Red—experiences engaged in, we recall, under the gaze of Popeye Vitelli. "I would write one," she says, "each time—afterward, after they—he left, and sometimes I would write two or three when it would be two or three days between when they—he wouldn't—" (148). In this comment, we can detect three properties of the imagination as Temple understands it. For Temple, the imagination is transgressive, libidinal, and memorial. Its function is to permit one to reexperience lost and forbidden pleasures by reconstituting them in words. As Temple says in explaining why she hired Nancy Mannigoe, the illicit nature of her life with Red meant that once "it was all over . . . it had to be as though it had never happened" (153). But the disappearance into silence of the memory of Red, she says, "was even worse" (153) than the loss of Red himself. Hence she hires "an ex-dopefiend nigger whore" (158) to help her reanimate in words her forbidden but treasured memories.

Turning from Temple Drake to Gavin Stevens is like turning from night to day. Faulkner suggests that it may be useful to think of Stevens in relation to the imagination in his first stage direction when he says that Stevens "looks more like a poet than a lawyer and actually is" (48). How this "poet" understands the function of the imagination can be inferred from the whole course of his interaction with Temple. His view contrasts with hers on a point-by-point basis. Where she associates the imagination with libidinal pleasure, he associates it with ethics and morality; where she uses the imagination to return to the past, he insists that it be used in the service of the future; and where she assumes that the purpose of the imagination is to preserve and renew desire, he assumes that its purpose is to free the mind of passion, by producing an act of catharsis.[4]

The contrast between Temple's and Gavin's views gains significance when we realize that they constitute two dimensions of Faulkner's own understanding of the function of the imagination, and that these dimensions exist in chronological relation to one another. A view of the imagination (and of artistic creativity) similar to Temple's appears in Faulkner's fiction of the 1920s and 1930s. In *Mosquitoes*, for example, Dawson Fairchild says that "about all the virtue there is in art" is that "it reminds us of youth" and hence permits us to "remember grief and forget time" (319). Elsewhere, Fairchild describes the artist as the person who is more willing than others to enter "the dark room" that Havelock Ellis and Sigmund Freud "have recently thrown open to the public" (248, 251). And throughout the novel, as in his reminiscence of his childhood encounter in the outhouse with the girl with the blonde curls, Fairchild associates beauty and artistic creativity with tabooed thoughts and activities.[5] But to find statements of Gavin Stevens's view of the imagination, we must turn from the works of the 1920s and 1930s to the public pronouncements Faulkner was making around the time of *Requiem for a Nun*—pronouncements such as the Nobel Prize Speech (1950), the Foreword to *The Faulkner Reader* (1953), and the Address to the Graduating Class at Pine Manor Junior College (1953). In the Nobel Prize Speech, for example, Faulkner specifically proscribes the association of the imagination with libidinal pleasure—here called "the glands"—and instead insists on associating it with the heart, the soul, and the spirit. Here too, he turns the imagination away from the past and toward the future, first by saying that the artist who writes of the glands "will write as though he stood among and watched the end of man," and then by saying that "the poet's voice need not merely be the record of man, it can be one of the props, the pillars to help him endure and prevail" (*Essays* 120).

This ameliorative view of the function of the imagination expresses the desire for rapprochement we detected in *Go Down, Moses*. For a variety of personal and cultural reasons—advancing age, the creative blockage already alluded to, the challenge posed to the modernist ethos by World War II—Faulkner evidently felt the need, in Hemingway's phrase, "to [move] in on the side of the strongest battalions" (*Selected Letters* 807).[6] But the evidence of the Nobel Prize Speech notwithstanding, the emergence of this view does not mean that Faulkner wished to repudiate his earlier, libidinally-oriented view. In fact, he argued that both views had always been present in his art. As he says in the Foreword to *The Faulkner Reader*, the desire "to uplift men's hearts" (*Essays* 180) was not absent from his earlier work but latent in it. When "the blood and glands and flesh still remained strong and potent," he says, the hope that his books might inspire people "was unimportant . . . as measured against the need to get them written" (180–181). But when "the blood and glands began to slow and cool a little," he suddenly saw that this hope had been present in his art "all the time" (181). Conversely, the new emphasis on this hope does not mean that he is "trying to change man" or that his art has become any less "completely selfish, completely personal" (181). Rather, trying to lift up men's hearts is simply a new way of doing what he had been trying to do in his earlier art, which is to "say No to death" (181).

In effect, then, in the early 1950s Faulkner was seeking to establish a complementary relation between the libidinal and the ethical dimensions of his art. He was searching for a way to allow the view of the imagination associated with Gavin Stevens to emerge into prominence without at the same time repudiating the view associated with Temple Drake and with his own earlier career. In his address to the graduating class at Pine Manor Junior College, he describes the form that such a complementary relation might ideally take. The core of the speech is an abbreviated creation story centering on a "splendid dark incorrigible" angel (*Essays* 137) who embodies the spirit of rebellion. The innovation that Faulkner brings to this story consists of splitting the dark angel's rebelliousness in half and of distinguishing between the effect on human history of the two halves. One of the halves—the dark angel's ambition—produces human woe, for from it springs "the long roster of the ambition's ruthless avatars—Genghis and Caesar and William and Hitler and Barca and Stalin and Bonaparte and Huey Long" (137). The other half, which Faulkner identifies as "the temerity to revolt and the will to change," produces human glory, for out of it comes "the long annal of the men and women who have anguished over man's condition . . . the philosophers and artists . . . who have reminded us always of our capacity for honor and courage and compassion and pity and sacrifice" (137–138).

In depicting the philosopher and artist as descendants of a primal act of Luciferian rebellion, Faulkner echoes William Blake's interpretation of the fall as the story of humankind's attempt to recover the power of the imagination from a jealous God.[7] But the purpose to which Faulkner directs this Blakean myth measures the distance he had travelled since his own youthful romanticism. In contrast to Blake's Imaginative Man, who is inherently transgressive, Faulkner's artists and philosophers serve surprisingly conservative ends. They do not direct their rebellion at God or nature or political institutions but at the fears and anxieties that prevent people from living comfortably in the world. Our aim in allowing "the poets and philosophers to remind us . . . of our capacity for courage and endurance" (138), Faulkner tells his audience of young women, is not to learn how "to be Joans of Arc with trumpets and banners and battle-dust" but to learn how to live happily within "the normal life which everyone wants and everyone should have" (139–140). If we devote our energies to achieving this normal life, which Faulkner here calls "home," we will find that we have overcome completely the dark angel's "ruthless and ambitious split-offs" (141–142).

The argument of the Pine Manor Speech provides an almost exact synopsis of the second act of *Requiem for a Nun*. Very nearly the whole objective of Gavin Stevens's long struggle with Temple Drake is to have her tell the story of her life in a new way, one which will not renew her illicit memories but will instead purge her of them and therefore make it possible for her to reassume her familial responsibilities. Central to this struggle is the name "Temple Drake." Toward the end of the first act of the novel, Gavin and Temple discuss whether "Temple Drake" or "Mrs Gowan Stevens" will visit the Governor. Temple wishes the visitor to be "Mrs Gowan Stevens" because "Temple Drake" is, in her view, the secret part of herself which "liked evil" (135) and which sought out opportunities to reconstitute her bordello experiences in language. Temple wishes to exempt this secret self from the conversation with the Governor because she cannot believe that retelling her story in an environment so alien to her former way of telling it can result in anything other than humiliation and suffering. Gavin Stevens, by contrast, wishes to involve "Temple Drake" in the conversation as fully as possible, for in his view only if Temple undergoes a cathartic reenactment of all of her shameful experiences (including the experience of reenactment itself) will she be able to transform herself into a willing wife and mother.

At first, the struggle between Gavin Stevens and Temple Drake seems to result in Temple's conversion to Gavin's way of seeing. This transformation occurs in three stages, the first of which consists of a dance of psychological evasion in which Temple engages during the first half of her visit to the Governor's office. In all its elements, this dance reflects Temple's resistance to Stevens's way of understanding the function of the imagination. Temple enters the Governor's office saying that the retelling is "not for anything" (152). It is "just suffering," and its effect will not be cathartic but emetic, "like calomel or ipecac" (152). Similarly, she treats every incidental detail of her encounter with the Governor as a symbol of her despair, converting the offer of a cigarette into a joke about a firing squad, and viewing the handkerchief extended in anticipation of her tears as if it were a blindfold for the execution this firing squad is about to perform. Also, she treats her secret identity in this same despairing way, pretending that "Temple Drake" is a separate being, to be referred to in the third person, as "Temple Drake, the white woman, the all-Mississippi debutante" (120) and "Temple Drake, the foolish virgin" (130).

Yet despite the ingenuity of her effort at evasion, Temple undergoes a slow shift in outlook as she tells her story. Like a patient in a therapeutic session who attempts to recount a traumatic event without emotion, Temple gradually loses her defensiveness and her capacity for self-alienation as her story advances. First she accepts the cigarette and handkerchief; then she begins speaking of herself and "Temple Drake" as if they were the same person; and finally she moves, hesitantly but inevitably, to an account of the core secret on which her self-loathing is founded. Significantly, this secret does not consist of her rape, or of her perjury against Lee Goodwin, or of her sexual experiences with Popeye and Alabama Red, but of her hiring Nancy Mannigoe to help her relive her libidinal memories. Other than the account of her child's murder, this is the fact about her past that Temple evades telling longest and that she recounts with the most emotion.

A moment's reflection should convince of the rightness of Faulkner's decision to place this secret at the end of the initial stage of Temple's development. All of Temple's other secrets are simply events from the past, and they presumably can be retold repeatedly without altering the emotion—whether of pleasure or of loathing—that accompanies them. But Temple's reliving of her sexual experiences in her conversations with Nancy is not simply an event *from* the past but a way of relating *to* the past. Recounting this secret, then, opens to the possibility of change not just the content but the structure of Temple's imagination. This Temple herself indicates, both in her inchoate resistance to voicing this secret and in her reaction immediately afterwards, when for the first time in the novel she speaks of the possibility of a cathartic function for the act of retelling, saying that the Catholic Church's sacrament of confession, if properly used, might eliminate "the maladjustments which they tell us breed the arsonists and rapists and murderers and thieves and the rest of the anti-social enemies" (159).

Once Temple shows herself to be receptive to the possibility of catharsis, the second and third stages of her development follow in rapid succession. The second consists of Gavin Stevens's replacement of Temple as speaker. Early readers of the novel tended to view Stevens's interruptions of Temple as attempts by an inexperienced dramatist to distribute essentially narrative material among his characters.[8] But the line of argument I am following here suggests that Stevens's emergence as speaker has a thematic function. His voice replaces Temple's because she has developed to the point where her outlook is ready to merge with his. Whereas Stevens's earlier attempts to interrupt and guide Temple had been greeted with objections by the Governor, after Temple tells of her conversations with Nancy the Governor invites Stevens to speak. As he does, a new, redemptive version of Temple's story comes into being. In this version, "the letters were not first. The first thing was the gratitude" (161). Seemingly secure in her role as wife and mother, Temple had actually been trapped inside a spiralling obligation to display gratitude to her husband for having been gentlemanly enough to marry her. When this fact is taken into account, Stevens suggests, Temple's behavior can no longer be interpreted as the product of an innate affinity for evil. Instead, it must be seen as noble, even heroic, for she has managed to hold together her family for six years while juggling "three glass bulbs filled with nitroglycerin": the need to offer atonement, the need to receive forgiveness, and the need to offer gratitude in response to the forgiveness (164–165).

Stevens's reinterpretation of the meaning of Temple's past encompasses even her recounting of her illicit memories. Far from being tawdry, semi-pornographic acts of self-titillation, Temple's conversations with Nancy must be viewed as attempts to "slough away the six years' soilure of struggle and repentance and terror to no avail" (170). Indeed, these recollections can even be construed as acts of love, for Temple's experiences with Alabama Red are the closest that her sad history ever permitted her to come to "honeymoon" and to "the similitude of being wooed" (169–170).[9] From this radical reinterpretation of the meaning of Temple's acts of recollection, it is an easy step to the final stage of her transformation, which consists of the flashback scene depicting the events surrounding the murder of her infant child. This scene completes Temple's turn toward catharsis both in its content, which presents a much more sympathetic view of Temple than she had presented earlier, and in its form. As Temple's completion of the scene in her own voice indicates, the flashback must be understood to be a dramatic enactment of her response to Gavin's final words: "Now tell him" (172). In shifting representational modes in this way, Faulkner creates a formal analogue for Temple's transformation in outlook. Underlying this shift is the assumption, common to our culture, that drama stands in a more immediate and authentic relation to experience than narrative. Hence replacing Temple's voice with a dramatic enactment of the content of her speech symbolizes the completion of her journey toward self-renewal. Beginning with evasions, lies, and acts of self-alienation, Temple here arrives at a moment of self-integration and self-acceptance, a mystical fusion of voice and action, past and present, memory and imagination.

II

Read in this way, the struggle between Gavin Stevens and Temple Drake reveals itself to be a meditation on the imagination, how impaired and restored. There can be little doubt that the climax of this meditation, with its promise of an integration of libido and superego, spoke to a very deep need within Faulkner himself, particularly at this stage in his career. Yet the second act does not end with Temple's flashback, but instead returns to the present time of the story and to the revelation that Temple's husband, rather than the Governor, had listened to her confession. As this scene develops, evidence rapidly accumulates that the supposed cathartic function of the flashback scene has at best been incompletely realized: Temple emerges from the flashback saying "still no tears" (195) and alluding once again to a cigarette as an emblem of an impending execution; and at the end of the scene she and Gavin Stevens revert to the idea, which she had expressed earlier, that her future will consist of repetition without progression, when Temple says "tomorrow and tomorrow and tomorrow," and Stevens responds, "he will wreck the car again against the wrong tree, in the wrong place, and you will have to forgive him again, for the next eight years until he can wreck the car again in the wrong place, against the wrong tree—" (206).

The reason Faulkner carries the action of the drama in this direction is not far to seek. Touching as it is, Temple's turn toward a cathartic view of the imagination is radically incomplete, for it does not carry the question of the purpose of catharsis beyond merely short term, utilitarian considerations. If the dramatic portion of the novel ended with the flashback scene, we would be left with a superficially appealing but ultimately unsatisfactory view of the imagination as simply the handmaiden of therapy—as nothing more than a way of arriving at a condition that Faulkner elsewhere in the novel dismissingly calls "eupepsia" (145). The whole tendency of Faulkner's mind, his insistence on pressing his thought beyond conventional limits and on exposing its ultimate, even eschatological, implications, argues against his ability to rest content with such a limited view of the function of the imagination. If the cathartic view of the imagination is to justify itself, it must do so under more severe conditions than those provided by an easy, optimistic appeal to the idea of mental health.[10]

Faulkner depicts these more severe conditions in the third act of the novel, in Temple and Gavin's visit to Nancy Mannigoe. As I suggested at the beginning of this chapter, it is difficult to arrive at a satisfactory interpretation of Nancy's role in *Requiem for a Nun*. But her function in relation to the theme I am exploring is entirely unambiguous. She signifies the dream of a life free of the imagination—free, that is, of the need to exist in a mediated relation to either a past or a future condition of pure being. Faulkner indicates that Nancy carries this significance in three aspects of her characterization: her illiteracy, her blackness, and her religious faith. Throughout his career, Faulkner associates the idea of pure being with illiteracy and pre-verbalism. In *Mosquitoes*, for example, Dawson Fairchild says that "when you are young, you just be. Then you reach a stage where you do. Then a stage where you think, and last of all, where you remember" (231). When a person reaches this last stage, he says, "you dont have thoughts in your mind at all: you just have words in it" (231). Later in his career, Faulkner challenges Fairchild's view, instead inclining toward the belief, now associated with Jacques Derrida, that the notion of pure being itself has no existence outside language. But he never loses his inclination to associate this idea (whether viewed as reality or as illusion) with illiteracy and pre-verbalism. Furthermore, perhaps because of the relatively high incidence of illiteracy among blacks in the pre-modern South, Faulkner frequently expands this association to include blacks as well. Time and again in his fiction, we see him suggesting that black experience—wordless black experience—may be more authentic than white experience and that blacks may have access to "a Oneness with Something, somewhere" that is denied to whites (*Soldiers' Pay* 319).[11]

This set of associations receives its fullest expression in Faulkner's fiction at the moment when Temple emerges from the flashback scene and begins to contemplate the question of her future. She immediately draws a lengthy contrast between how people react when a white person and when a black person enters "a jail or a hospital" (196). In the case of the white person, Temple says, "before you even know it, you have sent them books to read, cards, puzzles to play with" (197). But when the patient or inmate is black, "You dont even think about the cards and puzzles and books. And so all of a sudden you find out with a kind of terror, that they have not only escaped having to read, they have escaped having to escape" (197). The implication of Temple's contrast (and its application to her situation) should be clear. White people read, she suggests, because they are doomed to the Sisyphean task of attempting to reconstitute in words a lost condition of being. But blacks, by virtue of their illiteracy, have never fallen into the world of representation; they have escaped having to escape. Hence they are "serene and immune to anguish" (197). When one looks up at the window of the jail, Temple says, if the hands that appear are white, they will be "tapping or fidgeting or even holding, gripping the bars" (197). But if they are black, they will "just [be] lying there among the interstices, not just at rest, but even restful" (197).[12]

Illiteracy and blackness, then, are two of Temple's names for the dream of pure being. When this dream is projected into the future, beyond the life of representation, it carries another name. Then it is called "heaven." In the third act of *Requiem for a Nun*, in Temple's conversation with Nancy Mannigoe, Faulkner poses the hard question of whether the cathartic imagination can carry Temple forward into this condition, or at least into a secure enough belief in its existence to make her life bearable. The key term here is "belief," which Faulkner places in tension throughout the third act with the word "hope." One might expect that a conversion from despair to hope, could Temple achieve it, would be sufficient confirmation of the efficacy of the cathartic imagination. But in ultimate terms, such a conversion in outlook would simply reverse the direction of Temple's dilemma; it would merely shift the focus of effort and expectation and desire, to use Wordworth's definition of hope, from the past to something evermore about to be. This Nancy Mannigoe fully understands. Hence her insistence on associating hope with sin. "Hoping," she says, is "the last thing of all poor sinning man will turn aloose" (272). "You mean," says Gavin Stevens, "when you have salvation, you dont have hope?" (272). "You dont even need it" (273), says Nancy. "All you need, all you have to do is just believe" (273). Nancy does not say why the believing individual can dispense with hope, but we can readily supply the reason. The believer does not need hope because he or she exists outside time and beyond desire. Like "heaven," "belief" is a name we give to the dream of oneness with God—which is to say, to the dream of pure being imagined as a future possibility.

In setting Temple on a quest for an existence free of the need for hope, Faulkner makes an extreme demand on the idea of catharsis. Not satisfied with a notion of catharsis as an occasional period of release within an ongoing dialectic of desire, Faulkner requires that the concept justify itself in ultimate terms, by enabling the imagination to encompass itself, consume itself, and free the mind of itself. One suspects that a desire for this sort of imaginative self-transcendence was a frequent visitor to Faulkner's mind during the 1940s and early 1950s. We see traces of it in his recurrent assertion (the first in his career) of belief in God, in his concern (also new) with the relation between art and immortality, and in his frequent statements that he wished to break the pencil and cease writing.[13] But however strong this desire might have been, it was outweighed by an even stronger sense of skepticism. Neither Faulkner's belief in God nor his concept of immortality is personal in nature, and his most frequent term for the state of the individual beyond death is not "heaven" (or "hell") but "oblivion." Similarly, his most deeply held view of the purpose of the imagination is not that it should conduct us to an other-worldly condition of pure being but that it should, in the phrase already quoted, "say No to death." The artist, he says, is "everyone . . . who has tried to carve . . . on the wall of that final oblivion beyond which he will have to pass . . . 'Kilroy was here.'"[14]

Faulkner's skepticism has two effects on the dramatic sections of *Requiem for a Nun*. The first is that it causes him to leave Temple's quest for pure being in a state of unresolved ambiguity. Temple seeks the answers to three questions in the last act of the novel: whether she can believe, what she is to believe, and how she is to act. Nancy Mannigoe offers no practical help in answering any of these questions. In response to Temple's desperate final expression of doubt—"suppose tomorrow and tomorrow, and then nobody there, nobody waiting to forgive me" (283)—Nancy simply repeats her insistence that Temple must enter into an absolute condition of unqualified belief. But whether Temple—or anyone other than Nancy Mannigoe—can manage this feat, Faulkner does not tell us. At the end of the novel, he shows us Temple saying that without belief she is doomed and damned, but he does not show her saying that she has attained belief. Instead, he suggests in her last line—the single word "coming," spoken to her husband (286)—that she may simply be reentering without alteration the world of effort and expectation and desire.

The second, and for my purposes more important, effect of Faulkner's skepticism is that it prevents him from ever completely subordinating his transgressive, backward-looking view of the imagination to his ethical and progressive view. Had we known to look, we could have seen Faulkner rescuing the first of these views from incorporation into the second in the flashback scene itself. In the middle of this scene, Pete, Alabama Red's brother and Temple's lover, offers to return to Temple the packet of letters that has served as the basis of his blackmail. Temple takes the packet to the fireplace and threatens to burn it. The whole logic of the cathartic movement of the dramatic sections demands that Temple fulfill her threat, for the letters are the central symbol of the attitude she must relinquish if she is to reintegrate herself into home and family. Temple instead returns the packet to the table. With this gesture, the letters evade assimilation into the cathartic labor of regeneration and renewal. Slightly later, Faulkner carries the symbolism of the decision not to burn the letters a step further, when in a stage direction he says that "Pete . . . goes to the table . . . and with almost infinitesimal hesitation takes up the packet of letters [and] puts it back inside his coat" (180). Pete then passes out of the room and out of the novel. We never see him again because he has completed his role in Faulkner's meditation on the function of the imagination. With his departure, Temple's letters—and, we may add, "letters," writing, art—return to the possession of the outlaw, while the labor of catharsis looks forward only to tomorrow and tomorrow and tomorrow.

III

But what was this backward-turning imagination to feed on? This question required Faulkner's attention in the early 1950s for both internal and external reasons. Internally, as my argument suggests, the question arises because of Faulkner's fear that the libidinal subject matter of his earlier art—the "blood and glands"—was receding into inaccessibility. Externally, it arises from his sense that his other great subject matter—the sights, sounds, smells, and customs of his native region—was also disappearing. As we have seen, Faulkner anticipated this second disappearance fairly early in his career, in his brief note on *Flags in the Dust* and his unpublished introduction to *The Sound and the Fury*. By the time of the writing of *Requiem for a Nun*, these earlier statements must have seemed like prophecies whose time of fulfillment had arrived. In the postwar world depicted in this novel, Faulkner says, the idea of the South as "one irreconcilable fastness of stronghold" has become little more than "a faded (though still select) social club or caste"; it is a "form of behavior" that one only remembers to observe "on the occasions when young men from Brooklyn, exchange students at Mississippi or Arkansas or Texas Universities, [vend] tiny Confederate battle flags among the thronged Saturday afternoon ramps of football stadia" (246–247).[15]

The prose sections of *Requiem for a Nun* combine an elegaic account of this second, external disappearance with an exploration of its implications for Faulkner's art. Central to both these concerns is an elaborate array of images of language. The descent into a debilitating and destructive modernity that we examined in Chapter One is depicted in all three prose sections as a fall out of an original Edenic condition. This fall has several starting points, so that at various times we are shown the destruction of the South as the fall of the wilderness into civilization, as the fall of the settlement into the town, as the fall of the pre–Civil War world into the post–Civil War world, and as the fall of the nineteenth into the twentieth century. Accompanying this descent in all its phases is a contrast, similar in significance to the contrast between Nancy's illiteracy and Temple's literacy, between an unfallen and a fallen language.

It should not surprise us to find that the unfallen half of this contrast consists of signs etched directly into the surface of the world. The external equivalent of the dream of pure being is the dream of an unmediated interfusion of the self and the world. Like his romantic forebears, Faulkner tended to express his interest in this dream in images of inscribed writing. Throughout his fiction, he repeatedly invokes a representational hierarchy in which signs incorporated into the surface of the world—whether in the form of words or of nonverbal signifiers—are accorded greater force and authenticity than either speech or handwritten or printed writing. (One thinks, for example, of the many tombstones and signposts in his fiction, and of the high place he assigns sculpture in comparison to the other arts.) These observations explain why examples of inscribed language appear so prominently in the descriptions in *Requiem for a Nun* of each of the beginning stages of the South's fall into modernity. In pre-history, inscribed language appears as the "recessional contour lines" left behind by the ice age on "the broad blank mid-continental page" (99–100); much later, it appears as "the toed-in heelless light soft quick long-striding print" of the Indians' moccasins in the "dusty widening" that will become Jefferson (215, 220); and still later, it appears as "the fragile and indelible signature" etched by Cecilia Farmer on the jailhouse window in 1861 (229).[16]

As the South descends into the modern age, this original, unfallen language gradually comes to be supplanted by a debased alternative. Faulkner depicts this change in two ways. The first consists of a series of acts of erasure and overwriting. In the prose sections, Faulkner repeatedly suggests that the march of history erases or washes away the unfallen signs originally inscribed on the surface of the South, and that new signs are continually being written over the old ones. Thus the advance of white civilization replaces the print of the Indians' moccasins with insignia of its own, first by allowing "the pioneers, the long hunters" to step "into the very footgear of them they dispossessed," then by requiring the Indians to wear "the alien shoes" sold at the general store, and finally by encouraging the arrival of a steadily accelerating stream of "land speculators and . . . traders in slaves and whiskey" who print "deeper and deeper the dust of that dusty widening, until at last there [is] no mark of Chickasaw left in it any more" (218–220).

The second way Faulkner depicts the shift from an Edenic to a fallen language is through an overlapping series of associations between fallen writing and imprisonment. The disappearance of the Indians from the South occurs not only because of their physical departure for Oklahoma but also because of their enclosure in a text. Among the "miniscule of archive" (3) housed in Ratcliffe's store is "a ruled, paper-backed copybook . . . in which accrued . . . in Mohataha's name . . . the crawling tedious list of calico and gunpowder . . . drawn from Ratcliffe's shelves by her descendants and subjects and Negro slaves" (21). Once the Indians become inscribed in this book, their physical departure is virtually assured. Long before Faulkner depicts this departure, however, he creates a further association between writing and imprisonment, by saying that the documents pertaining to the dispossession of the Indians are enclosed in "a sort of iron pirate's chest" (3). From this association further associations follow, as the iron chest disappears inside the lean-to courthouse attached to the jail, and Alec Holston's "ancient monster iron padlock" (3) undergoes a "transubstantiation" (9) into the new, permanent courthouse. So finally the world symbolized by the Indians (along with their ability to inscribe their experience directly onto the surface of the South) can be said to be enclosed in a text that is inside a chest that is inside a building that is itself a transformed version of a lock.

Faulkner's equation of the South's descent into modernity with the erasure, overwriting, and imprisonment of an unfallen language suggests an obvious parallel to his own situation as a recently blocked artist. Perhaps surprisingly, it also points toward a liberating alteration in his understanding of his art that was taking place in the early 1950s. To see how this is so, we need to compare the attitudes toward time expressed in the prose and the dramatic sections of the novel. The prose sections lack the intense fascination with an ameliorative view of the future that we found in the dramatic sections. In the dramatic sections, Gavin Stevens and Temple Drake struggle over the question of whether Temple is journeying through a tunnel or into a barrel, up a hill or toward a precipice. In the prose sections, the answer to this question is never seriously in doubt. In the short term, Yoknapatawpha County and the South are heading mindlessly toward complete assimilation into the "W.P.A. and XYZ" (243) of an anonymous federalism. In the long term, the nation as a whole is heading with similar mindlessness toward apocalypse: America, Faulkner says, is a "towering frantic edifice poised like a cardhouse over the abyss of the mortgaged generations" (247); driven by "a furious beating of hollow drums toward nowhere" (4), it is whirling "faster and faster toward the plunging precipice of its destiny" (226).

The extreme pessimism of this view of America's future explains why the prose sections of the novel do not include any significant attempts to alter the course of history. With only minor exceptions, Faulkner depicts no public, collective acts of resistance to the juggernaut of modernity. He does, however, depict a private form of resistance, one which grows in the course of the third prose section into a metaphor for the change occurring in his art. This private form of resistance consists of the defiant nostalgia with which single individuals or small groups of individuals greet each major step in the modernization of the South. First Alec Holston turns his face toward the wall during the founding of Jefferson and the departure of the Indians for the West; then a group of "aging unvanquished women" defy reconstruction by "facing irreconcilably backward toward the old lost battles, the old aborted cause (239); and finally a few "irreconcilable Jeffersonians and Yoknapatawphians" insist, in the mid-twentieth century, "on wood-burning ranges and cows and vegetable gardens and handymen who [have] to be taken out of hock on the morning after Saturday nights and holidays" (251).

Faulkner's central agency for the expression of this defiant nostalgia is the jail, which enacts a turn back toward the past through its ability to watch, remember, and record the history of Jefferson. For most of the third prose section of the novel, the jail's nostalgia appears as unlikely as that of Alec Holston and the other irreconcilables to stem the tide of modernity. But as I argued in Chapter One, the last third of "The Jail" depicts a countermovement in which the "rush and roar of . . . progress" (247) is not merely stemmed but dispelled. In the terms I am pursuing here, this countermovement can be said to reside in the jail's immunity to erasure and overwriting. Whereas change affects the rest of the county as an obliterating flood, the "ephemerae of progress and alteration" merely wash across the surface of the jail "in substanceless repetitive evanescent scarless waves" (250). Consequently, the jail is able to carry undamaged into the modern world, and make available for a liberating act of reading, a fragment of unfallen language—the signature of Cecilia Farmer inscribed on one of its windows. When the stranger reads this signature, he learns "that there is no time: no space: no distance" (261). "All you had to do," Faulkner says, "was to look at [the signature] a while; all you have to do now is remember it." Do either, and Cecilia Farmer's "clear undistanced voice" will repeat once again its original, unfallen, undying message: "*Listen, stranger; this was myself: this was I*" (262).

In effect, then, the prose sections of the novel espouse the same view of the relation of the imagination to time as the dramatic sections: in both, Faulkner rejects an ameliorative, progressive view and reaffirms his original association of the imagination with the past. At first glance, this reaffirmation might appear to answer by force of will the question I posed a few pages ago—the question of what Faulkner's imagination was to feed on. In a limited sense, this impression is correct: in assigning an act of reading the power to overcome time, Faulkner implies that it might be possible to recreate by fiat the southern culture whose passing he had chronicled. But Faulkner was too clearsighted an artist to devote his energies to this antiquarian project. Instead, he searched for and discovered a more workable way of allowing his imagination to remain allied to the past.

The nature of this more workable way can be inferred from a change that occurs midway through the stranger's act of reading. When Cecilia Farmer's signature first begins to stir the stranger's imagination, he asks for an account of the few facts still known about her life. The account he receives causes him to engage in an act of historical reconstruction, as he finds himself "watching and hearing" (256) Cecilia's husband-to-be on the occasion of her first glimpse of him. But this reconstitutive use of the imagination, compelling though it is, reveals its inadequacy almost immediately. First the stranger exhibits a need to go beyond the few known facts about Cecilia by supplying a color for her hair. Then he rejects the conventional interpretation of her subsequent history as a "long peaceful connubial progress toward matriarchy" (258–259). Although he knows that Cecilia left Jefferson with her husband-to-be, he decides that "bridehood, motherhood, grandmotherhood, [and] widowhood" are "nowhere near enough" for the person he has begun to see in his mind; this person, he says, is "fatal instead with all insatiate and deathless sterility; spouseless, barren, and undescended"; she is "demon-nun and angel-witch; empress, siren, Erinys: Mistinguette, too" (258–261).[17]

Implicit in this startling reinterpretation of Cecilia's story is a new way of viewing the relation of the imagination to the past. By interpreting Cecilia's story as freely as he does, the stranger suggests that he is less interested in her signature as a historical record than as a fictional text. He is not content simply to use Cecilia's act of writing as a way of recovering the experience it encodes (if indeed this is even possible); he wants to read the signature in a writerly fashion, to use Roland Barthes's term. He wants to read it in a way that will foreground the availability of the signature—the text—to multiple, even contradictory interpretations. As we see in the stranger's equation of Cecilia with Mistinguette, who was not even born until 1875, this writerly form of reading does not reject meanings that could not have been intended when the text was written. Refusing to privilege the relation of a past text to past experience, the stranger views Cecilia's story as something that lives and grows in time, accruing new meanings as it comes into contact with new experiences and new readers.[18]

As with the stranger, so with Faulkner himself. In 1945, midway through his long period of creative blockage, Faulkner wrote the addendum to *The Sound and the Fury* called "The Compson Appendix." In the Appendix, Melissa Meek, the Jefferson town librarian, discovers a photograph depicting Caddy Compson in the company of a German staff general. After keeping the picture locked away in the library for a week, Melissa journeys to Memphis to ask Dilsey Gibson to help her save Caddy. But Dilsey, who in *The Sound and the Fury* had said "Ive seed de first en de last . . . I seed de beginnin, en now I sees de endin" (371), refuses to look at the picture, saying "My eyes aint any good anymore . . . I cant see it" (418). On her way back to Jefferson, Melissa understands the real reason Dilsey did not look at the picture. It is because Caddy, the character Faulkner always spoke of as if she were his muse, "*doesn't want to be saved hasn't anything anymore worth being saved for nothing worth being lost that she can lose*" (420). So Melissa, presumably still carrying the picture, returns to the library, where "life [was] lived too with all its incomprehensible passion and turmoil and grief and fury and despair, but here at six oclock you could close the covers on it and . . . put it back . . . on the quiet eternal shelves and turn the key upon it" (419).[19]

In *Requiem for a Nun*, Faulkner accepts the vision of his artistic future he had glimpsed in "The Compson Appendix." He allows his art to enter the library. In turning his imagination back toward the past, Faulkner was not seeking to recreate a lost southern culture, or even his own past libidinal experiences. He was attempting to renew his creativity by engaging in a writerly reading of a group of literary texts. These texts are his own earlier works of fiction. In *Requiem for a Nun*, for the first time in his career, Faulkner makes his own past artistic achievement the subject of his art—in the dramatic sections by making Temple's story an extension and revision of *Sanctuary*, and in the narrative sections by retelling parts of the Sartoris, Compson, and Sutpen stories and by reusing some of the language of *Go Down, Moses*. In turning to this subject matter, Faulkner discovered the central artistic strategy of the final phase of his career, for in *The Town*, *The Mansion*, and *The Reivers*, he repeatedly makes similar use of his earlier fiction. The elegaic tone of *Requiem for a Nun* suggests that Faulkner did not willingly choose this artistic strategy: only a fragment of unfallen language speaks at the end of "The Jail," not a full text, and the message it whispers is "*this was I*," not "*this is I*." And certainly, as many critics have told us, this strategy entailed a risk, not always as successfully overcome as in *Requiem for a Nun*, of self-parody and self-repetition. But in comparison to the alternatives exercised by so many of his artistic coevals—suicide, alcoholism, silence—Faulkner's decision to enumerate old themes can be seen to be life-affirming—even, if I may hazard the term, therapeutic. O joy! that in our embers is something that doth live.

FIVE

The Scene of Instruction

On December 5, 1942, William Faulkner wrote a long letter congratulating his step-son, Malcolm Franklin, on his decision to enter the armed forces. Four months later, he wrote a similar letter to his nephew, James Faulkner, who by that time had already enlisted in the Marines (*Selected Letters* 166, 171). These letters are among the earliest examples we have of Faulkner explicitly taking on the role of tutor to the young. Although he apologizes in the one for writing a "sermon" and in the other for writing in a "preachified" manner, clearly in each he is responding to a heartfelt need to teach. He thereby broaches an important theme of both his life and his art during the second half of his career. In his life, the impulse to teach appears most clearly in his service as a university lecturer and as a State Department cultural representative, but it can be seen as well in his brief dream of founding and directing a colony for young artists and in his decision to use part of his Nobel Prize money to provide college scholarships for black students. As for his art, time and again in the fiction of the 1940s and beyond we observe the prototypical scene of an older man obliquely but insistently attempting to teach a young person, usually an adolescent. Most often the older man is Gavin Stevens and the young person is Charles Mallison, but many other pairings occur as well: Sam Fathers and Ike McCaslin in *Go Down, Moses*, Lucas Beauchamp and Mallison in *Intruder in the Dust*, Stevens and Temple Drake in *Requiem for a Nun*, the General and the Corporal in *A Fable*, Stevens and Linda Snopes in *The Town*, and Grandfather Priest and Lucius Priest in *The Reivers*.

To an extent, Faulkner's late interest in teaching expresses an impulse present throughout the whole of his adult life. As Joseph Blotner and others have argued, Faulkner the writer-in-residence and author of novels depicting teaching descends from Faulkner the scoutmaster and deviser of ghost stories and other entertainments for children.[1] Certainly this view expresses a share of the truth; but it will mislead us if it prevents us from noticing that Faulkner also displayed a deep and abiding resistance to education. He failed to complete high school and achieved only mixed success as a special student at the University of Mississippi. In his later years, he consistently—albeit humorously—referred to himself as a "veteran sixth grader" (*Essays* 219) and refused to accept any form of academic honor. Throughout his fiction, he mocks the figure of the other-worldly scholar, and in both *The Sound and the Fury* and *Light in August* he depicts the miseducation of the young with a ferocity reminiscent of Dickens's *Nicholas Nickleby*, Butler's *The Way of All Flesh*, and Joyce's *Portrait of the Artist as a Young Man*. When viewed in relation to this history, Faulkner's late inclination to teach and to depict scenes of instruction gains considerably in interest. It reveals itself to be the outgrowth of a complex internal dialogue, one involving central questions about Faulkner's attitude toward patriarchal values and beliefs, toward a liberal, progressive vision of human experience, and toward his own development as an artist. In this chapter, I will explore this dialogue, first by examining the theme of resistance to education in *The Sound and the Fury* and *Light in August*, then by speculating on the meaning that this resistance held for Faulkner, and finally by tracing its influence on the scenes of instruction in the late novels.

I

On the last morning of his life, Quentin Compson prepares three envelopes. The first contains a note telling his roommate, Shreve MacKensie, to allow Deacon, the unofficial "guide mentor and friend" of Harvard freshmen, to have a bag containing Quentin's old suit and some other articles of clothing (*Sound and the Fury* 92–93, 112). The second, which Quentin takes with him when he leaves the dormitory room for the last time, is also addressed to Shreve; it evidently contains a suicide note. The third, which Quentin mails to his father, contains the key to the trunk in which he has packed the remainder of his possessions. The key is wrapped in a blank piece of paper. Quentin's ostensible purpose in mailing this third envelope is to complete the pattern of dutiful behavior that has always characterized his relations with his parents. As with his waiting until the end of the purchased year at Harvard to commit suicide, his dutifulness takes the form of economic prudence. By mailing the key to his father, Quentin ensures that his possessions will not be lost or stolen, and hence that his suicide will not entail any unnecessary waste.

Yet like many suicidal gestures, Quentin's mailing of the key carries a heavier burden of meaning than perhaps he intends. The trunk that the key unlocks invites comparison with the coffin that will need to be returned to Jefferson after Quentin's death, should his body be recovered. Quentin himself frames a similar association early in the second section of the novel when he remembers the preparations for Mrs. Compson and Caddy's journey to French Lick and thinks "*Bringing empty trunks down the attic stairs they sounded like coffins French Lick. Found not death at the salt lick*" (108–109). In both instances, the association of trunk and coffin reveals the resentment toward his parents that Quentin's dutiful behavior only half-conceals. The ironic conjunction of the coffin image and the phrase "*found not death at the salt lick*" succinctly expresses Quentin's view of the journey to find a husband for Caddy as an interring of his sister within the death-in-life of Mrs. Compson's obsession with respectability; and his scrupulous regard for the well-being of his possessions when he himself is on the threshold of death suggests that he holds a similar view of his own situation. Forced to go to Harvard against his own wishes, he senses that his desires are of less importance to his father than is his usefulness in placating his mother's neurotic demands. Hence Quentin takes pains to preserve the useful—that is, the material—residue of his year at Harvard while casting aside his now-useless self. But the sedulousness with which he performs this last service ensures that the resentment underlying it will not remain concealed. The key he sends his father unlocks nothing of real value, while his failure to write words of explanation or affection on the enclosing sheet of paper inscribes it with a silent statement of his anger (cf. Watson, *William Faulkner: Letters and Fictions* 80–83).

Quentin's resentment of his father reveals itself in a variety of other ways, most notably in the challenge to his father's authority implicit in his fantasy of confessing that he and Caddy had committed incest. In attempting to explain this resentment, critics have tended to assimilate it to the history of generational decline so prominent in many of Faulkner's other Yoknapatawpha novels. In this view, Quentin resents his father because he has inherited the shell of his family's aristocratic code of honor without its substance. Because Mr. Compson cannot measure up to the standard of greatness established by his own father and grandfather, the argument goes, he retreats into bibulous cynicism and fails to provide his son with a model of parental behavior that will allow Quentin to grow into adulthood and to assume parental authority in his own right (see Irwin, *Doubling and Incest* 67–70; Bleikasten, *The Most Splendid Failure* 109–116 and "Fathers in Faulkner" passim).

We see grounds for this interpretation in the emphasis Faulkner gives to the declining material fortunes of the Compson family and to Mr. Compson's inability to protect Caddy from her mother's mania for respectability. But grounds also exist for doubting its exclusive validity. We should note, for example, that Faulkner gives much more attention to the

Compson generations preceding Mr. Compson's in the Appendix he wrote in 1945 and in his retrospective comments on *The Sound and the Fury* than in the novel itself. In the novel proper, very little attention is paid to events prior to the birth of the Compson children, and almost nothing is said that romanticizes either the family's past or southern history. More important, by assimilating Quentin's resentment to the history of generational decline this mode of interpretation valorizes patriarchal values in the very act of examining a challenge to them. Because Quentin resents his father, we are told, he must necessarily want a more authoritative father than the one he has. His resentment is compromised at the outset by being interpreted as a form of frustrated love, and the subversive thrust of the novel's vision of father-son relationships is blunted by being subordinated to a generalized nostalgia for a lost patriarchal order.

This last consideration is of paramount importance to our understanding not only of Quentin's relation with his father but of other parent-child relationships in the fiction of the late 1920s and 1930s. In Faulkner's great novels, nostalgia for a lost patriarchal order is never evoked unequivocally; it always comes accompanied by a radical critique of the ideology of fatherhood—and, more generally, of parenthood. This critique is essentially ahistorical in its thrust: in its unelaborated form, it views all parenthood as a repetitive, self-generating fiction that derives its authority from nothing more than the accidental priority of the parent over the child. We sense the existence of this critique in Darl's monologues in *As I Lay Dying* and, as Patricia Tobin has shown, in the Sutpen story in *Absalom, Absalom!* (107–132). We sense its existence as well in Faulkner's deliberate and repeated misalignments of familial functions and roles. Faulkner's families consistently enact the distinction that R. D. Laing draws between family and "family"—between, that is, family as a set of blood ties and "family" as a set of functional relationships (3–19). Because authorial sympathy in these enactments is repeatedly directed toward the child and away from the parent, Faulkner's fiction hollows out parenthood. Mrs. Compson may be Benjy's biological mother, but Caddy and Dilsey are his functional ones, and Mrs. Compson's emotionally self-serving appeals to her maternal prerogatives and feelings serve only to reveal the spuriousness of her claim to the title of "mother."[2]

Faulkner's critique of parenthood renders problematic the idea of instruction. However indirectly, most teaching involves a transfer of power between generations and therefore presupposes the existence of altruistic impulses in the teacher and of a willingness to learn in the pupil. In part of his being, Quentin desperately wants such a transfer to take place. Beneath his metaphysical pretensions he is an adolescent, with an adolescent's characteristic mixture of desire for adult capacities and of embarrassment over not already possessing them; and throughout the last day of his life he displays a continual, although sidelong, interest in the ways his contemporaries are making the transition into adulthood. Looking out his dormitory window at students hurrying to chapel, he reflects on Spoade's casual, "senior" attitude—so unlike his own—toward the college's rules and regulations. Although not a smoker, he buys a cigar after breakfast and tries to smoke it; later in the day he recalls in precise and envious detail Dalton Ames's ability to roll a cigarette, to strike a match with his thumb, and to blow smoke through his nose. Returning to the dormitory after his fight with Gerald Bland, he displays an agonized adolescent self-consciousness in the steps he takes to prevent people from seeing his black eye; and in the last act we see him perform, he pauses to put on his hat before leaving to commit suicide so that other students won't think he is "a Harvard Square student making like he was a senior" (205).

This distaste for adolescence and desire for adult power and knowledge helps to explain why Quentin so frequently envisions his father in the role of instructor and himself in the role of student. Throughout his recollections of their conversations, he assiduously attends to his father's apothegms and explanations, as if hoping to learn from them the secrets of adulthood. Yet in another and more dominant part of his personality, Quentin deeply distrusts all education. His sense of the inauthenticity of his parents' lives combines with his fear of time and sexuality to create a despairing sense that learning the lessons of adulthood will destroy, rather than deepen, the meaning of his existence. He views education, in its public, institutional forms, as a source not of liberation but of repression, and he resists it internally even while outwardly displaying the characteristics of a good student. Of his childhood schooling he remembers only his almost erotic longing for the schoolday's end, and he is so indifferent to the educational aspects of his Harvard experience as to fail to mention any professors he has known, classes he has taken, or knowledge he has gained.[3] And in his relation with his father, a similar undermining takes place. Although he assigns his father the role of instructor and himself the role of student, he tries to restrict the lesson he will learn to the circuit of his own backward-turning desire, demanding that his father teach him only how to be free of the need to be taught. Thus the conversation that dominates Quentin's memory just before he leaves the dormitory room for the last time takes on the quality of a mock tutorial, in which instruction is offered but rejected: "you are still blind," says Mr. Compson, "to what is in yourself to that part of general truth the sequence of natural events and their causes which shadows every mans brow even Benjys"; to which Quentin replies, sullenly, "nobody knows what i know" (203–204).

In his distrust of education, Quentin reminds us of Joe Christmas, the hero of Faulkner's other ironic Bildungsroman. In *Light in August*, in fact, resistance to instruction and the critique of parenthood it implies are more prominent than in *The Sound and the Fury*, for they are freed of the ambiguities that accompany their presentation in the earlier novel. The distinction between family and "family," for example, is even more central to Joe Christmas's situation than to Quentin's. It reveals itself in Christmas's childhood in the dietician's abandonment of her professional role of nurturer (itself a parody of parental nurturing) and in the narrowing down of Christmas's opportunities to receive maternal affection to the single pathetic instance of his relationship with the twelve-year-old orphan girl, Alice. It is emphasized as well in Christmas's adolescence, both by Mr. McEachern, who refers to Mrs. McEachern as "your fostermother" (154) ten years after Christmas's adoption, and by Christmas himself. Similarly, the mixed fearsomeness and desirability that characterizes adult knowledge in *The Sound and the Fury* is here reshaped into a single monolithic form. In *Light in August*, adult knowledge is entirely repressive and life-denying, a single-minded obligation to "fear God and abhor idleness and vanity" (134), and its symbol is a series of closed and incomprehensible books: the "enormous Bible with brass clasps and hinges and a brass lock" (137) on the table in the McEachern house, the Spanish Bible out of which Calvin Burden reads to his uncomprehending son, the Presbyterian catechism which McEachern expects Christmas to study. And just as adult knowledge is stripped of its ambiguity, so is its intended recipient freed of uncertainty. Quentin's inward-turning intellectualism makes all things, including his attitude toward parental knowledge, shadowy and paradoxical. But for the essentially unreflective Christmas, the issue is clear: McEachern's knowledge is false, his parenthood fictitious, and both are to be adamantly resisted.

Yet neither Joe Christmas nor Quentin Compson is able to avoid the onset of knowledge. For both characters, the act of resistance derives its shape from the knowledge they seek to avoid. Quentin's dream of freedom from time and sexuality is a mirror reflection of his father's despairing attitude toward the future, and even his distrust of education gains much of its substance from his father's skepticism: Mr. Compson, we recall, describes Harvard as a place "where the best of thought . . . clings like dead ivy vines upon old dead brick" (109) and he chooses his son's graduation from high school as the occasion to give him a watch he calls "the mausoleum of all hope and desire" (86). In much the same way, Joe Christmas's attempts to resist his foster-father's religious instruction create a corresponding zealotry of denial. When he and McEachern walk to the barn midway through a Sunday morning of attempted instruction, there is "a very kinship of stubbornness like a transmitted resemblance in their backs" (139); and when Christmas stands in the barn, silently refusing to study the catechism, he takes on first "a rapt, calm expression like a monk in a picture" and then an "attitude . . . of exaltation" like that of a "Catholic choir boy" (139–140). Similarly, his reactions against his childhood scenes of instruction in his later life serve only to reenact them. He beats McEachern's horse as he himself was beaten, he rejects Joanna Burden's food as he had rejected Mrs. McEachern's, he kills Joanna Burden when asked to kneel and pray.[4]

II

The scenes of instruction in *The Sound and the Fury* and *Light in August* depict education as an unavoidable imposition, an act of betrayal wherein an adult inscribes his or her inauthentic image on a vainly resisting child. In these novels, education is a form of psychic violence, an invasion, as Addie Bundren says in *As I Lay Dying,* of the "secret and selfish life" of children by the cold adult belief that the purpose of living is to learn how "to stay dead a long time" (161–162). What personal experiences impelled Faulkner to take such a narrow and negative view of education may never be entirely known, although the evidence we have of his father's intermittent alcoholic rages and his mother's emotional rigidity and perfectionism suggest that his own childhood experiences of parental instruction may not have been happy ones. But it is significant that with the writing of *The Sound and the Fury* Faulkner began to associate resistance to instruction with the deepest sources of his art and that he located these sources in the earliest stages of psychic development. As Jay Martin has argued, Faulkner's adolescent resistance to formal schooling can be interpreted as a rebellion against his mother, who valued education very highly. As Martin also argues, this rebelliousness reemerges in the writing of *The Sound and the Fury,* where it takes the form of a rejection of the repressive, perfectionist view of art Faulkner had espoused in the early 1920s and of a deliberate regression into a sensual and self-absorbed relation with the products of his imagination. Evidence that Faulkner was aware of the nature and significance of this rebellion can be found in the introduction to *The Sound and the Fury* written in the summer of 1933. In this introduction, Faulkner frames a link between his discovery of the self-absorbed, asocial element of his art and the idea of resistance to instruction.

This link reveals itself in the description of the genesis of *The Sound and the Fury* in the longer of the two versions of the introduction. In the shorter and presumably later version, Faulkner says, as he does repeatedly throughout the rest of his career, that the novel began for him with the image of the Compson boys looking up at Caddy's muddy drawers as she climbed the pear tree outside the room where their grandmother lay dead. In the earlier, longer, and more self-revealing version of the introduction, Faulkner gives much more emphasis to Benjy's role in the genesis of the novel. The instant when "the entire story . . . seemed to explode on the paper before [him]" (413), he says, was when he envisioned Caddy pausing from her play in the stream to comfort the crying Benjy. Coincident with this vision came the realization that "Benjy must never grow beyond this moment; that for him all knowing must begin and end with that fierce, panting, paused and stooping wet figure" (413). For Benjy, he says, the "grief of bereavement" must not be "leavened with understanding and hence the alleviation of rage as in the case of

Jason, and of oblivion as in the case of Quentin" (413). And later, in a remarkable characterization, Faulkner says that in order for Benjy to be "impervious to the future" he had to be "without thought or comprehension; shapeless, neuter, like something eyeless and voiceless which might have lived, existed merely because of its ability to suffer, in the beginning of life; half fluid, groping; a pallid and helpless mass of all mindless agony under sun, in time yet not of it . . ." (414).

The extraordinary accumulation of embryonic images in this characterization suggests that while for narrative purposes Faulkner needed to assign rudimentary intellectual capacities to Benjy, he actually envisioned him as if he were newly come from the womb. When so envisioned, Benjy can be seen to embody a stoppage of education—in the broadest sense of the term—at a point in time just beyond its outset. Faulkner's insistence on driving this stoppage back as close as possible to the beginning of consciousness suggests that he held a more radical view of Benjy than do many of his readers. From a conventional point of view, Benjy's idiocy is tragic because it prevents him from developing into a mature adult. For Faulkner, by contrast, Benjy's tragedy is not that he cannot learn but that he has already learned too much. Benjy's "grief of bereavement" must not be "leavened with understanding" because it expresses a universal human trauma (413). Like all of us, Benjy grieves over his subjection to the primal scene of instruction. Thrust into consciousness, he learns of separation and loss. Bereft of the unity of the womb, he momentarily finds compensation in his sister's affection, only to discover that "the dark harsh flowing of time [is] sweeping her to where she [can]not return to comfort him" (413). And in resistance to this knowledge, he moans and bellows.

In Benjy we see displayed Faulkner's understanding of the ultimate source of all resistance to instruction. The act of parental inscription on the mind of the vainly resisting child is here understood to begin with the infant's discovery of the otherness of its mother and hence of the existence of an inimical relation between itself and the world.[5] The vehemence and extravagence with which Faulkner explores this understanding in his great fiction is one of the main sources of its power; in the intensity with which he depicts the dissolution of the dream of primal unity, he shows himself to be a worthy heir of Milton and of Wordsworth. Yet in the context of his career as a whole, this intensity of vision was not without expense. In a sense, Faulkner can be said to have burned his bridges in advance of himself. To found one's art on recollection of loss and on resistance to change presupposes that in one's imagination one need never grow up—need never, that is, shift from identification with the child to identification with the parent. In his fiction of the late 1920s and 1930s, Faulkner brings his youthful characters to the edge of adulthood, only to fix them there, as if both for them and for him a chasm existed which could not be crossed. As Jean-Paul Sartre says in commenting on *The Sound and the Fury*, in his great fiction Faulkner writes as if the future did not exist ("On *The Sound and the Fury*" 91–92).

Then the whirligig of time brought in his revenges. After *Light in August*, Faulkner ceased to depict scenes of instruction for a considerable period; with the notable exception of *Absalom, Absalom!*, no such scenes occur until *Go Down, Moses* and the novels of the late 1940s and 1950s.[6] When these scenes reappear, they are the product of an altered—one might almost say, a chastened—sensibility. Throughout this book, I have argued the importance of Faulkner's mid-1940s period of creative silence to an understanding of his later career. During this period, Faulkner exhibits an intense concern over the impending onset of age and over the question of what is appropriate or possible behavior for a person of his years. In the last sentence of the letter to his stepson that I mentioned at the beginning of this chapter, he uses the words "old" and "older" five times in explaining why he will not himself be entering the armed services; and in his other letters from these years, he refers in a variety of ways to his new-found sense that time is beginning to close in on him. Yet frequently, often in the very same letters, he searches for ways to deny the importance of the passage of time. He gets out his RAF uniform and notes proudly that he can still button it; he says, half defiantly, that he hasn't "said at 42 all that is in the cards for me to say" (*Selected Letters* 125); and he expresses again and again a yearning for something different, something new, as if he hoped by some change in his circumstances to bring about personal rejuvenation.

As I have described it here, Faulkner's period of creative silence in the 1940s can be seen to display the characteristics of a mid-life crisis. It is not surprising, then, to find that Faulkner emerged from this time with a strong desire to engage in the mode of behavior Erik Erikson calls "generativity." Erikson uses this term to designate a mid-life stage of personality development in which an individual's attention shifts from a more-or-less exclusive preoccupation with establishing his or her own position in the world to an interest in "establishing and guiding the next generation" (267).[7] The term does not refer, I should emphasize, to child-rearing as such but rather to a more diffuse and generalized interest in providing guidance and counsel. For Faulkner, this interest appears to have originated in relation to his own family, but it quickly expanded to embrace the larger world. As he reluctantly admits in his letter to his stepson, World War II is for men younger than himself; it is they, not he, who must fight. But when the war is over, he says, "the time of the older men will come, the ones like me who are articulate in the national voice . . . and have been vocal long enough to be listened to" (*Selected Letters* 166). When that time comes, Faulkner implies, he will enter the public arena and begin to function as a teacher and sage.

But what exactly was he to teach? That all knowledge begins in loss? That instruction is an act of psychic violence? The transition into generativity contains an element of trauma in the best of circumstances, for it entails a tacit acceptance of one's own mortality (Jacques passim). For most people, though, the transition at least has the advantage of being continuous with the past, in that the knowledge they seek to impart is a residue of their own earlier creative endeavors. But for Faulkner, reentering the scene of instruction in the 1940s required that he make a series of fundamental breaks with his earlier self. In order to teach, he needed to relinquish his cherished reclusiveness, to reconstitute his art along more explicit lines, and—most important—to credit parenthood and other forms of authority with an authenticity he had formerly withheld from them. No more compelling evidence exists of Faulkner's tenacity of will than his undergoing this effort at self-revision. Yet clearly the attempt encountered deep internal resistance and achieved only partial success. Although in the 1940s Faulkner sincerely wished to become articulate in the national voice, he even more deeply wished to continue to be the self-absorbed and self-delighting artist he had discovered himself to be at the time of the writing of *The Sound and the Fury*. Because the emergence of the one desire coincided with the growing inaccessibility of the other, the move into generativity must have seemed, at times at least, to betray a central aspect of his artistic identity. Hence in his later career Faulkner approached both the act and the theme of instruction with deep equivocation.

III

Faulkner's equivocation is nowhere more evident than in *Intruder in the Dust*. Central to this novel is the education of its protagonist, Chick Mallison, into the painful moral complexities of adulthood. Although Faulkner depicts Mallison's education as successfully achieved, he also displays deep ambivalence about its methods, aims, and limits. The most obvious form that this ambivalence takes is an opposition Faulkner establishes between the means of Mallison's moral growth and institutional education. Like his fictional precursor, Ike McCaslin in *Go Down, Moses*, Mallison faces a moment of crisis in which he must choose between learning and schooling. Just as Ike must skip school if he is to learn what Sam Fathers's death has to teach him, so Mallison must play truant for a day if he is to pursue his attempt to rescue Lucas Beauchamp to its climax. Mallison's decision to do so contributes to both his emotional and his moral growth. In emotional terms, Faulkner presents the choice between school and truancy as a choice between infancy and adulthood: for Mallison and Gavin Stevens at least, the insistence that Mallison attend school on this crucial day has its origins in Mallison's mother's "refusal to forgive [him] for being able to button [his] own pants" (*Intruder in the Dust* 107), while their joint decision to participate in the reopening of the grave seems to them an act of adult self-assertion. In moral terms, the issue posed by the decision to play truant is even more acute, for institutional education reveals itself to be an agency of the social order whose authority and rightness Mallison has begun to challenge; only by staying out of school can Mallison learn a lesson about his society that school, by its nature, must fail to teach him.[8]

By establishing an opposition between Mallison's moral growth and formal schooling, Faulkner suggests that true education is a private rather than a social act, a matter of learning rather than of being taught. The more closely we look at the means by which Mallison's education is accomplished the stronger this suggestion grows. In *Faulkner: The Transfiguration of Biography*, Judith Bryant Wittenberg observes that Faulkner inverts detective story conventions in *Intruder in the Dust* by relying not on "the anticipated ratiocination of the 'detectives'" to solve the crime but on "their antirationalism, their willingness to act while putting 'all thought ratiocination contemplation forever behind them'" (212). A similar observation can be made about Mallison's education. His most significant breakthroughs occur as a result not of instruction but of private moments of intuition. Furthermore, all of these moments entail acts of transgression. From his initial, tentative discovery that "*you dont have to not be a nigger in order to grieve*" (25), to his sensitivity to the look of "mute patient urgency" (66) on Lucas Beauchamp's face in the jail cell, to his acceptance of Miss Habersham as a partner, to his opening of the grave itself, Mallison's growth consistently arises from his willingness to transgress the moral and social boundaries established by conventional "wisdom."

The hidden question at the heart of *Intruder in the Dust*—and of Faulkner's equivocation over teaching—is when and why this process of subversion should end. In one sense, of course, it never should: in a letter written in 1952, Faulkner told his protégé, Joan Williams, "You have got to break your wall. You have got to be capable of anything, everything, accepting them I mean, not as experiments, clinical, to see what it does to the mind, like drugs or dead outside things, but because the heart and the body are big enough to accept all the world, all human agony and passion" (*Selected Letters* 338). This statement as much memorializes Faulkner's own past fictional practice as it advises an aspiring artist, for in his great fiction Faulkner created an enduring record of his willingness to transgress imaginative barriers. But as I argued in Chapter Four, in his later career Faulkner was not content to view the breaking of taboos as an end in itself, but instead strove to link imaginative transgression to ethical goals. The conversation between Gavin Stevens and Chick Mallison that dominates the last third of *Intruder in the Dust* is an equivalent in educational terms of this attempt. In it, Faulkner seeks to convert learning into teaching and subversion into social integration.

Yet when we read *Intruder in the Dust* in the context of Faulkner's earlier depictions of acts of instruction, we become aware of the difficulty he had in satisfactorily terminating Mallison's movement into transgression. Evidence of this difficulty can be found both in the nature of the teacher-pupil relationship depicted in the novel and in the content of Stevens's act of instruction. In *Intruder in the Dust*, as in his earlier novels, Faulkner displaces family into "family," in this instance by making Mallison's transition into adulthood the concern not of his father but of his uncle. As the shadowy presence of Charles Mallison, Sr. makes clear, this displacement is not without cost. Although Chick and Gavin Stevens both assume that Chick's mother will try to make him attend school the morning after the opening of the grave, his father actually does so. As Chick discovers, this effort is part of a campaign of "psuedo-scornful humorous impugnment of his and Aleck Sander's courage" (132); and as he soon realizes, this campaign occurs because "his father was gnawing the true bitter irremediable bone of all which was dismatchment with time, being born too soon or late to have been himself sixteen and gallop a horse ten miles in the dark to save an old nigger's insolent and friendless neck" (133).

In this comment, Faulkner allows us to peer into the emotional core of the scene of instruction. The mixed pride and envy with which Charles Mallison, Sr. responds to his son's act of courage reflects the ambiguous struggle for dominance between father and son that underlies encounters between male teachers and pupils and that makes them potentially so perilous. But in *Intruder in the Dust*, Faulkner chooses to displace this conflict to the margins of the novel's action. Although he acknowledges its existence in this brief encounter between father and son, he does not allow it to emerge, even in disguised form, in the relationship between uncle and nephew. This decision permits him to depict instruction as successful, but at the expense of narrowing its range of significance. Because the relationship between Chick Mallison and Gavin Stevens is represented as essentially ethical in character, rather than libidinal, Gavin Stevens's efforts at instruction encounter no resistance other than that provided by their subject matter. Nowhere are they impeded by the secret emotional agendas of either teacher or pupil. So abstracted and purified a concept of education threatens always to reveal its own hollowness: in comparison to Chick's father's desperate attempt to reduce his son's adventure to "a kind of kindergarten witchhunt," as Chick himself says, "it was his uncle's abnegant and rhetorical self-lacerating that was the phony one" (133).

Similar considerations apply to the content of Stevens's act of instruction. *Intruder in the Dust* contains an elaborate array of images of motion and stasis, of linearity and circularity, and of threatening or disquieting faces. One of the main references to motion—the iterated phrase "just dont stop"—forms the core of Stevens's message to his nephew. This phrase completes a triple pattern of movement consisting of Mallison's fantasied flight from Jefferson on his horse Highboy, of his actual journeys to Caledonia Chapel, and of his internal, metaphoric journey into moral adulthood. Ostensibly, Stevens's "just dont stop" says that the internal journey must never cease, that growth is a continual process of transgressing barriers.

Stevens's true purpose, however, is not continuation but closure. Mallison's initial fantasy of riding off "in a straight line in the opposite direction from Frazer's store" actually promises a reciprocal movement, for he intends to stay away from Jefferson only until the situation involving Lucas is "all over finished done" (41). But his two journeys to Caledonia Chapel cast into doubt the desirability of this intended return. As his surreal visions of Miss Habersham's drive home and of many faces merging into a single face together suggest, the flight of the county residents from Jefferson after the mystery has been resolved creates a corresponding impulse toward psychic flight in him. Just as Miss Habersham is separated from Jefferson by "that unpierceable barrier of rushing bumper-locked cars and trucks" (186), so Mallison is separated from Yoknapatawpha County by his vision of the county residents as "not faces but a face, not a mass nor even a mosaic of them but a Face: not even ravening nor uninsatiate but just in motion, insensate, vacant of thought or even passion" (182). The hidden purpose of Gavin Stevens's conversation with Mallison is to dissolve this alienating image into its familiar elements and thus to allow Mallison to reenter Yoknapatawpha County. In the novel's complex dialectic of motion and stasis, then, Stevens's "just dont stop" actually counsels stoppage. It teaches Mallison to cease the transgressive motion of thought once it reaches the point where it threatens to alienate him from his homeland.

A corresponding movement toward closure occurs in Stevens's discourse on race relations. Poised against Stevens's refamiliarization of the faces of the county residents is an earlier encounter with an alien face. When Mallison emerges from the icy stream on Edmonds's plantation, he looks up "at the face which was just watching him without pity commiseration or anything else, not even surprise—. . . a face which in his estimation might have been under fifty or even forty except for the hat and the eyes, and inside a Negro's skin but that was all . . . because what looked out of it had no pigment at all, not even the white man's lack of it" (6–7). As Faulkner's odd syntax suggests—a face inside a skin, out of which looks something more remote—Mallison here encounters the novel's central image of otherness. *Intruder in the Dust* records Mallison's efforts variously to repudiate this otherness and to acknowledge his secret affinity with it. Just before he makes the mistake of offering payment for the food he has eaten, Mallison pauses to look at "the gold-framed portrait-group" (14) in the corner of the Beauchamp cabin. The images of Lucas and Molly that look back at him "from behind the round faintly prismatic glass dome as out of a seer's crystal ball" (14) adumbrate the choice he faces, for they provide him with an opportunity to see in the cabin a form of life not unlike his own. When he instead senses that there is "something ghastly, almost intolerably wrong" (14) about the image of Molly because it shows her without her headrag, he demonstrates how deeply imbued he is with the outlook of his time and place and how far he needs to journey before he will be able to look into Lucas's face and see the "mute patient urgency" it contains (66).

Stevens's discourse seeks to terminate this journey. It does so most obviously in the notorious Sambo image Stevens uses on the drive out to Caledonia Chapel. This image (and the argument with which Stevens surrounds it) slows Mallison's rebellious rush into identification with Lucas by substituting a type for an individual and by replacing the issue of a specific injustice with the larger and more ambiguous question of race relations in general. A similar but more subtle closure of Mallison's moral journey resides in the nature of the amelioration of the racial problem that Stevens envisions. Stevens's argument co-opts not only Mallison's need for racial justice but also his youthful need for rebellion. By saying that Southerners "alone in the United States . . . are a homogeneous people" and by arguing that they "must resist the North" so that they may themselves have "the privilege of setting [Sambo] free" (153–154), Stevens seeks to socialize rebellion. He encourages Mallison to view reintegration into Yoknapatawpha County not as a craven acquiescence to an adult sense of expediency but as a heroic continuation of his adolescent quest for separateness. In effect, Stevens's argument replaces the alien Face of Yoknapatawpha County against which Mallison has begun to define himself with the "countless row on row of faces" that Mallison imagines as looking down at him from the "curving semicircular wall" separating North and South (152). It replaces Mallison's real adventure of subversive growth with the southern boy's fantasy of being present at the Battle of Gettysburg and of perhaps even reversing its outcome (194–195).

The difficulty with this argument, as Faulkner recognizes, is that the vision of southern homogeneity it offers Mallison is spurious. *Intruder in the Dust* is haunted almost to the point of obsession by the image of a landscape void of blacks. Although this absence can be accounted for in plot terms by the black inhabitants' fear of being caught up in the expected revenge against Lucas, it has a deeper imaginative significance as well. This significance is revealed midway through Mallison and Stevens's journey to Caledonia Chapel, when Mallison gazes out of the car window at the fields in which no black sharecroppers or tenant farmers are to be found. Absent from this landscape, the narrator says, is "the land's living symbol—a formal group of ritual almost mystic significance . . . tying the county-seat to the county's ultimate rim as milestones would: the beast the plow and the man . . . tremendous with effort yet at the same time vacant of progress, ponderable immovable and immobile like groups of wrestling statuary set against the land's immensity" (147).

As Faulkner's language suggests, the absent "formal group" of black farmer, mule, and plow is an icon of pastoral timelessness; like the plow silhouetted against the sky in Willa Cather's *My Ántonia,* it expresses the dream of an agrarian world exempt from time and change. Yet as Faulkner well knew, southern blacks had already begun to vacate this dream. Faulkner expresses his awareness of this fact in *Requiem for a Nun,* when he speaks of the departure of "an entire generation of farmers" (245) from the South. "Time was," he says, "when the mule stood in droves at daylight in the plantation mule-lots across the plantation road from the . . . two-room shotgun shacks in which lived in droves with his family the Negro tenant- or share- or furnish-hand who bridled him" (245). But in the postwar world both have departed, the mules "to the last of the forty- and fifty- and sixty-acre hill farms" and the blacks (nine out of ten of them at least) "to New York and Detroit and Chicago and Los Angeles ghettos" (245). These departures have occurred, Faulkner says, because the development of mechanized farming means that the tenth black can do the work of the other nine; by "mounting from the handles of a plow to the springless bucket seat of a tractor, the tenth Negro dispossess[es] and displac[es] the other nine just as the tractor had dispossesed and displaced the other eighteen mules to whom that nine would have been complement" (245).

But if this is so, then Stevens's vision of a South "not only impregnable but not even to be threatened" (156) represents less actuality than desire. Setting Sambo free is not a privilege Stevens can retain for the South, because it has been preempted by the real process of historical change occurring in the postwar world. Yet Faulkner cannot simply have Stevens urge Mallison to participate in this process, for this would require that he interpret positively the emergence of a deregionalized, urban, technological modernity. Furthermore, it would be tantamount to acknowledging the disappearance of Yoknapatawpha County as a viable artistic subject matter—a disappearance which, as we have seen, Faulkner had great reason to fear at this point in his career. Stevens must instead teach the illusion of a homogeneous South. He must teach it because otherwise Faulkner cannot confine Chick Mallison's subversive journey into adulthood within the boundaries of Yoknapatawpha County.[9]

IV

In effect, then, Faulkner's attempt in *Intruder in the Dust* to express his urge toward generativity encountered two interrelated obstacles. On the one hand, it was impeded by his reluctance to invest the scene of instruction with its full psychosexual complexity; on the other hand, it was impeded by the conflict between his desire to teach a liberal, progressive ethical lesson and his desire to hold on to the Yoknapatawpha County of his youth. The other novels of the late 1940s and early 1950s—*Knight's Gambit*, *Requiem for a Nun*, and *A Fable*—exhibit similar irresolution. In each of them, Faulkner explores the option of subordinating his art to his ethical didacticism. But because this possibility met with such severe internal resistance, it was never fully enacted. Instead, the novels of this period focus simultaneously on instruction and on the impulse to revolt against it; Faulkner's true subject during this time is his equivocal movement toward and away from the desire to teach. The bleakness of *A Fable* (where efforts at instruction tend to end in death) suggests that by the mid-1950s this dance of equivocation had begun to pall for Faulkner. To do anything more with his desire to teach, and with education as a theme, he needed to find a different way of approaching the scene of instruction. This he discovers in *The Town.* In this novel, Faulkner largely abandons his attempt to ethicalize his art. Instead, he aestheticizes teaching.

This change is part of a larger one that occurred toward the end of Faulkner's career. As many readers have observed, Faulkner's last three novels exhibit a more relaxed and contemplative outlook on life than do the earlier postwar novels. It is as if the working-through process observed in *Requiem for a Nun* had completed itself, allowing Faulkner to accept changes in himself (and in the South) that he had formerly tried to defy. In terms of the theme of education, this relaxed sense of acceptance takes the form of an emphasis on the affinities between art and teaching rather than on their differences. Instead of opposing art to teaching and requiring himself to choose between them, Faulkner suggests that both are, in Jacques Derrida's term, supplementary activities. That is, he suggests that art and teaching are both ways in which human beings seek to compensate themselves for loss. As the poet chews his "bitter thumbs" over the disappearance of some form of perfection and then reenacts in writing the grief occasioned by the loss, so the teacher attempts to construct in the pupil—the "little doll" of the Latin etymology of the word—the image of a vanished fullness.[10]

In *The Town,* Faulkner explores this affinity through the figure of Gavin Stevens, who is not only Linda Snopes's teacher but also the novel's most articulate exponent of ideas about art. The exploration begins with Stevens's first extended encounter with Eula Varner Snopes. When Stevens goes to his office to meet Eula the night after the Cotillion Ball, he still hopes to contend with Manfred de Spain for her favors. He learns in the course of the encounter not only that this hope is in vain but also why he will never succeed in wooing Eula.

The reason, Eula says, is that he spends "too much time expecting" (94), where "expecting" means "thinking" and "imagining" as opposed to "feeling" and "doing." Stevens himself concurs in this judgment. Throughout his encounter with Eula, he displays a troubled awareness of her gaze, which he describes as "that blue envelopment like the sea" (92). His mingled fascination with and fear of her gaze betokens a larger doubleness in his reaction, for though he sees in Eula a promise of complete and unbridled libidinal release, he also fears the loss of self-possession and self-awareness that sexual intercourse with her would entail. Hence he cries "Dont touch me!" and says, "So if I had only had sense enough to have stopped expecting, or better still, never expected at all, never hoped at all, dreamed at all . . . it might have been me instead of Manfred? But dont you see? Cant you see? I wouldnt have been me then?" (94).

Once Stevens acknowledges his concurrence in his own libidinal inhibition, he is ready to assume the dual role of teacher and of figure of the artist. After his encounter with Eula, he withdraws from his struggle with Manfred and decides to go "to that German university he had been talking for two years now about what a good idea it would be to go to . . . providing you happened to want to go to a university in Germany like that one" (101–102). In making this decision, Stevens enacts a link he had already established between education and sublimation, for earlier he said that he had failed to notice Eula because he "had been too busy passing bar examinations to have had time to prone and supine myself for proper relinquishment" (91). When he returns from Germany and World War I eight years later, he substitutes education for libido in earnest: no longer a pupil, he becomes a teacher when he sees Linda Snopes for the first time since her childhood and begins the extended process of "forming her mind" (179).

Stevens states his motive for his attempted education of Linda in the section of his narrative immediately following his first sight of her as an adolescent. After quoting an approximation of Housman's "And now the fancy passes by, / And nothing will remain," Stevens says, "which, praise the gods, is a damned lie since, praise, O gods! Nothing cannot remain anywhere since nothing is a vacuum and vacuum is paradox and unbearable."[11] Instead of "nothing remaining, it is Remaining which will always remain, never to be completely empty of that olden anguish" (135). As long as "the blood at least will always remember that once it was that capable, capable at least of anguish" (135), Stevens will know that he is alive. Hence he teaches Linda as a way of remembering his earlier brush with libidinal fulfillment. In teaching her he makes her "my child and my grandchild both"; and because "the McCarron boy who begot her . . . in that lost time, was Gavin Stevens in that lost time . . . Gavin Stevens is fixed by his own child forever at that one age in that one moment" (135–136).

Approached in this way, teaching joins art as a form of compensation: just as "the weak and impotent and terrified and sleepless that the rest of the human race calls its poets" work to reincarnate "brave virgin passion" (226) so does Stevens in his teaching. By moving teaching and art into alignment, Faulkner frees himself to depict the art of instruction in a fashion consistent with his new mood of relaxation and self-acceptance. Where in *Intruder in the Dust* Stevens directs his efforts as a teacher at containing Chick Mallison's rebelliousness within the boundaries of Yoknapatawpha County, he here tries to release Linda to the larger world: he acknowledges that "it was Jefferson itself which was the mortal foe since Jefferson was Snopes" (217), and he attempts to send Linda to a northern college. Similarly, where in *Requiem for a Nun* Stevens had sought to suppress Temple's libidinal writing and speaking in favor of the self-restraint of family life, he here seeks to reinforce the link between libido and writing: he gives Linda the poems of "Jonson and Herrick and Thomas Campion" (204), and he achieves his final triumph by freeing her to live in the Bohemian world of Greenwich Village.[12]

In *The Town*, then, Stevens's acts of instruction encourage a loosening of social and ethical constraints. For some readers of Faulkner's late fiction, this encouragement is less complete than it ought to be. As Irving Howe says of *The Mansion*, "Only at the end of the novel, as Stevens and Linda kiss goodbye and he slides his hand down her back, 'simply touching her . . . supporting her buttocks as you cup the innocent hipless bottom of a child,' does Faulkner break into the candor for which this whole section cries out" (292). Implicit in this criticism, for many contemporary readers at least, is an awareness that Faulkner's life exhibited the "candor" his fiction lacks—that in his love affair with, and attempted tutelage of, Joan Williams he sought to walk in April again both sexually and artistically. But in the final analysis, *The Town* is less concerned with Faulkner's relationship with Joan Williams (or with Jean Stein) than with the relationship's aftermath. The novel records Faulkner's rueful acknowledgment of the impossibility either of "being 21 again" or of recovering his artistic greatness by "taking his love and creating a poet out of her" (Blotner, *Faulkner: A Biography* 1293, 1303).[13]

In the terms I am pursuing here, this acknowledgment means rejecting the temptation to believe that either art or teaching can return one to a lost state of fulfillment. Gavin Stevens faces and surmounts both forms of this temptation in the concluding chapters of *The Town*. On the evening of his last encounter with Eula Varner Snopes, he drives out to a ridge "beyond Seminary Hill" (315); while there, he enacts one of the most famous representations of the figure of the artist in all of Faulkner's fiction, as he looks down at Yoknapatawpha County and sees in it "the sum of [his] life" and "the record and chronicle of [his] native land" (315–316). At first glance, this scene may seem to depict a single, fixed image of the artist, but it actually depicts a movement between two contending images. At the outset of the scene, Stevens envisions himself as a godlike, Joycean artist, indifferent to his creation. Referring to himself in the second person, he says that "[you are] detached as God himself for this moment above the cradle of your nativity" (316). Thinking of himself in this way allows Stevens to imagine that he can "preside unanguished and immune above this miniature of man's passions and hopes and disasters" (316). But the temptation to occupy a position of godlike superiority soon passes; in the remainder of the scene, Stevens descends by stages into an awareness of what he calls the "premature" (317) quality of life. As "you, the old man, already white-headed" stand on the ridge, he says, "there rises to you, about you, suffocating you . . . the spring darkness, the spring weather" (317). This weather is "the cup, the bowl proffered once to the lips of youth and then no more; proffered to quench or sip or drain that lone one time and even that sometimes premature, too soon. Because the tragedy of life is, it must be premature, inconclusive and inconcludable, in order to be life; it must be before itself, in advance of itself, to have been at all" (317–318).

This descent into an awareness of the irretrievability of lost libidinal fulfillment allows Stevens to accept his supplemental status, both as an artist and as a teacher. Stevens went to the ridge after receiving the note asking him to meet with Eula because he wanted to ask "*Why me? Why bother me? Why cant you let me alone?*" (318). The answer, implicit in his contemplation of Yoknapatawpha County, is that "bother," in the sense of the anguish of recollection, is inherent in life. Thus, when he descends from the ridge and meets with Eula, he accedes to her request that he assume the burden "of a young abandoned girl's responsibility" (335). And when Eula kills herself, he insists on functioning as an artist in relation to her memory, for as Ratliff says, "it was him—Lawyer—that helped Linda hunt through that house and her mother's things until they found the right photograph and had it—Lawyer still—enlarged, the face part, and sent it to Italy to be carved into a . . . yes, medallion to fasten onto the front of the monument, and him that the practice drawings would come back to to decide and change here and there and send back" (349; Faulkner's ellipses).

To complete this acceptance of his supplemental status, Stevens must overcome a last temptation, one centered on his role as teacher. At their final meeting, Eula repeatedly asks Stevens to marry Linda. In declining her request, Stevens reenacts an earlier scene, one that is itself a reenactment of an even earlier event in his life. When Matt Levitt, Linda's boyfriend, blows the horn of his homemade racer outside the Mallison house, tears the pages out of a gift book of poetry, and beats Stevens, he echoes events in Stevens's failed effort to contend with Manfred de Spain for Eula's favors. But the outcome of the second series of events reverses that of the first, for after Levitt beats Stevens, Linda slaps Levitt and rushes into Stevens's arms. Stevens then asks her to marry him. When Linda agrees, Stevens faces the central crisis of his career as a teacher, for her willingness encourages him to believe that a teacher can find in a pupil not just a simulacrum of lost fulfillment but fulfillment itself. Stevens resists this temptation, both here and when Eula renews it at their final meeting. The reason he gives Eula for refusing to marry Linda—"Put it that I'm not too old so much as simply discrepant" (332)—places full weight on the word "discrepant." Gavin Stevens has learned in the course of the novel that life is founded on discrepancy, on the discontinuity between representation and presentation, art and experience, youth and age. The most he can hope for, either as an artist or as a teacher, is not to recover the past but to remember it.

V

In *The Town*, Faulkner comes closer than anywhere else in his fiction to transferring allegiance from the figure of the student to the figure of the teacher. Yet one comes away from the novel with the impression that this transference is at once too complete and not complete enough. It is too complete in the sense that Faulkner's identification with Stevens as teacher does not leave room for any residual identification with Linda as pupil. We never learn what Linda thinks of the journey into freedom that Stevens has prepared for her, nor are we even given the sense that the question is an important one to ask. The transference is not complete enough in the sense that Faulkner's use of a male-female teacher-student relationship allows him once again to bypass the struggle for libidinal dominance that is at the heart of his depictions of the scene of instruction in his greatest fiction. When Linda says to Stevens just before her departure from Jefferson that Flem Snopes is not her father, Stevens tells the lie about Linda's legitimacy that Eula had asked him to tell, and he tells it so plausibly that Linda believes it. Here, as in *The Sound and the Fury* and *Light in August,* a teacher instills a patriarchal fiction in the mind of a student, but he does so without encountering the fierce resistance that accompanies attempts at instruction in these earlier novels.

This resistance is absent, one suspects, not because Faulkner imagines that women acquiesce more readily than men to masculine authority but because a young woman's growth into sexual maturity does not challenge an older man's libidinal identity in the same way a young man's does. As the scenes in *The Mansion* of Stevens's involvement in the plans for Linda's marriage make clear, her sexual maturation provides a new opportunity for him to engage in the compensatory use of the imagination that began when he envisioned himself as Eula's first lover and Linda's father. The fiction of fatherhood that Stevens imparts to Linda at the end of *The Town* is thus a trope of his own continuing imaginative involvement with her. But were Stevens to send a young man—Chick Mallison, say—forth into the world, he would very probably not find surrogate libidinal gratification in the young man's sexual adventures. The scene of instruction between males is too unilateral to encourage this possibility: it does not afford an imaginary reenactment of the older man's desires but instead calls for the older man to step aside from the Oedipal struggle in favor of the younger.[14]

To complete his encounter with the scene of instruction, then, Faulkner would need to depict a male teacher successfully releasing libidinal control to a male pupil. He nowhere includes such a scene in his fiction; but at the end of *The Reivers*, he achieves an approximation of it. In *The Reivers*, Faulkner again depicts education as an oscillation between a parental desire to inscribe images of authority on the mind of a child and the child's need to engage in irregular and perilous acts of discovery. At the outset of the novel, Lucius Priest is firmly in the grasp of the first of these two ways of learning, for he spends his weekdays in school and his Saturday mornings learning the lesson of economic responsibility that his father wishes to impart to him. But when the death of his maternal grandfather and the departure of his parents and grandparents for Bay St. Louis create a temporary hiatus in the structure of parental authority, he begins a journey into the second kind of learning.

Like many other aspects of *The Reivers*, Lucius's journey into forbidden knowledge exhibits a strong element of retrospection. Ned McCaslin and Uncle Parsham Hood, for example, educate Lucius in a way similar to Lucas Beauchamp's instruction of Chick Mallison; and Miss Reba's house of prostitution again links knowledge and libido as it did in *Requiem for a Nun*. But the air of geniality with which Faulkner revisits these elements of his earlier fiction deprives them of their perilousness. The one serious question raised in the novel is not whether Lucius will return safely from his adventure but how he and his father will negotiate his reentry into the family. At first, it appears that they will repress the adventure and the kind of knowledge it provided. When Lucius returns home, he notes with dismay the lack of alteration in his surroundings. This absence of difference casts doubt on the significance of the experience he has undergone, for as he says, "if . . . the things I had done and seen and heard and learned that Mother and Father wouldn't have let me do and see and hear and learn . . . had changed nothing . . . then something has been wasted, thrown away, spent for nothing" (299–300). Hence he accedes to his father's attempt to rescind the experience by reinstating parental authority: when his father says, "Let's get it over with," Lucius replies "Yes sir" and follows his father to the basement for his expected whipping (300).

Yet both Lucius and his father recognize the futility of this attempt to reinstate parental authority. In Lucius's words, "if after all the lying and deceiving and disobeying and conniving I had done, all he could do about it was to whip me, then Father was not good enough for me" (301). As Lucius and his father contemplate their impasse, Lucius's grandfather suddenly intercedes to resolve it. By introducing the figure of the grandfather into this final scene of instruction, Faulkner puts a central motif of his earlier fiction to new use. In *Doubling and Incest/Repetition and Revenge*, John T. Irwin points out the importance in Faulkner's fiction of the fantasy Ernest Jones calls "the reversal of generations" (94–97). This fantasy consists of the belief, common among children, that they are their parents' parents. Chick Mallison describes the fantasy explicitly in *The Town*, when he says, "to the child, he was not created by his mother's and his father's passion"; instead, "he came first, before the passion; he created the passion, not only it but the man and woman who served it; his father is not his father but his son-in-law, his mother not his mother but his daughter-in-law if he is a girl" (305).

Both in Chick Mallison's description of it and in Faulkner's earlier uses of it in his fiction, the fantasy of the reversal of generations is a weapon in the Oedipal war between fathers and sons: imagining himself as his father's father (or father-in-law) allows the son to exact a sort of revenge for his father's priority over him.[15] But in *The Reivers*, Faulkner inhabits this fantasy not only from the point of view of a child but from that of an adult. Because Lucius is telling the story of his conversation with his grandfather to his own grandchildren in his old age, he is at once grandson and grandfather. Arching across five generations in this way permits Faulkner to break the cycle of repetition that arises from the father's inscription of the image of authority on the mind of the son. When Lucius's grandfather intercedes in Lucius's punishment, Maury Priest protests, saying, "No. . . . This is what you would have done to me twenty years ago" (301). Grandfather Priest replies, "maybe I have more sense now" (301), dismisses his son, and proceeds to teach Lucius not to suppress his new-won libidinal knowledge but to treasure it. In response to his grandson's question, "How can I forget it? Tell me how to," he says, "You cant . . . Nothing is ever forgotten. Nothing is ever lost. It's too valuable" (302). Instead, he says, Lucius needs to "live with it," which he will be able to do if he can learn the further lesson of how to be a gentleman, because "a gentleman can live through anything" (302).

In this conversation, Faulkner reaches a graceful and relaxed resolution not only to *The Reivers* but to his career-long concern with the scene of instruction: if fathers cannot freely teach, perhaps grandfathers can. Yet we should note that this resolution, relaxed as it is, is not quite the novel's final word on the theme of education, for here as throughout his career Faulkner allows his fiction to elude the closure he appears to be imposing on it. Fittingly, this last evasion of closure takes the form of a reentry of the father into the scene of instruction. On the day after his conversation with his grandfather, Lucius notes one last consequence of his rebellious journey when he says, "Father wouldn't let Mother write me an excuse, so I had to take the absent marks. But Miss Rhodes was going to let me make up the work" (303). Dismissed from the scene of his son's instruction by his own father, Maury Priest reenters it in this prohibition. Muted, displaced, and made comic, the father's effort to teach his son the lesson of repression still continues.

EPILOGUE

The Poetics of Space

In a prefatory note accompanying *The Mansion,* Faulkner says that the novel "is the final chapter of, and the summation of, a work conceived and begun in 1925" (n.p.). The "work" referred to in this statement is the Snopes trilogy, which Faulkner began in the mid-1920s, with the writing of *Father Abraham.* But as several critics have observed, the prefatory note can also be interpreted in another way, for *The Mansion* attempts a summation not just of the Snopes trilogy but of aspects of Faulkner's career as a whole. Details such as Montgomery Ward Snopes's visit to Miss Reba's house of prostitution and Jason Compson's defeat by Flem Snopes in the Meadowfill affair provide evidence, as Michael Millgate says, that in the late 1950s Faulkner's "mind was turning toward a rationalizing review of his previous work" (252).[1] Among the several ways the novel supports this sort of reading, one is of interest to me here. In my opening chapter, I argued that the story of Linda Snopes Kohl and Gavin Stevens gains significance if read as a contribution to Faulkner's career-long meditation on the relation between his artistic identity, the South, and the modern world. In these closing comments, I wish to argue that the same is true of the story of Mink Snopes.

If I am to make this case, I first need to link together two of Faulkner's fictional settings, one of which has already made several appearances in these pages. Faulkner's career can be described with a fair degree of accuracy as an exploration of two settings: the mansion or plantation house and the jail or prison. Faulkner begins this exploration in *Flags in the Dust,* with a highly romanticized depiction of the "still and serenely benignant" (11) plantation house inhabited by the Sartorises. For the next ten years, in *The Sound and the Fury, Sanctuary, Light in August,* and *Absalom, Absalom!,* he devotes a considerable amount of energy to dismantling this romantic image. As this dismantlement reaches its climax, jails, prisons, and prison-like settings emerge into prominence, first in *The Wild Palms* and *Go Down, Moses,* then in almost every one of the postwar novels.

This shift in settings is not adventitious. It is another axis along which Faulkner enacts the double journey into loss that is the central theme of this book. In *Flags in the Dust,* Faulkner depicts the Sartoris plantation house both as a symbol of a vanishing social order and as a site for acts of visionary seeing. Throughout the novel, the plantation house enables its inhabitants to engage in nostalgic reverie by affording them protection from the intrusions—both literal and metaphoric—of the modern world. We can see in this circumstance an analogy to Faulkner's artistic self-understanding at this stage in his career, for both thematically and stylistically *Flags in the Dust* is largely an exercise in nostalgia. It attempts, as Faulkner said, "to recreate between the covers of a book [a] world . . . I was already preparing to lose and regret" (Blotner, "William Faulkner's Essay" 122), and it makes this attempt in a style that hearkens back to the comprehensiveness, omniscience, and narratorial self-assurance of the nineteenth-century realistic novel.

The breakthrough in vision and method Faulkner achieved in writing *The Sound and the Fury* consists in large measure in his moving his art outside this protected space. The passing of an aristocratic social order that is still only a melancholy possibility in *Flags in the Dust* is in *The Sound and the Fury* an accomplished fact. Similarly, the authoritative point of view used in the earlier novel disappears entirely. *Flags in the Dust* is filled with images and acts of comprehensive seeing: the Sartoris house commands a view of "the cradling semicircle of hills in panorama" (13); the effigy of John Sartoris in the Jefferson cemetery gazes out "upon the valley where for two miles the railroad he had built ran beneath his carven eyes" (351); Young Bayard looks down from "the cold peak of his stubborn despair" on "the warm, sunny valleys where people lived" (230). But in *The Sound and the Fury,* comprehensive vision disappears. A major cause of our sense of claustrophobia in the first three sections of the novel is our inability to see anyone or anything clearly. Quentin may notice "the rim of white under [Caddy's] irises" (174) and Jason "her lip jerking higher and higher up her teeth" (239), but not until the fourth section of the novel do we receive a comprehensive description of any character or setting. And even in the fourth section, as André Bleikasten says in *The Most Splendid Failure,* the point of view "is neither that of an all-seeing and all-knowing narrator nor that of a detached and strictly objective observer" (175). It is instead reticent, tentative, and conjectural, couched in terms of "as if" and "as though," of "seemed," "appeared," and "might have been" (176; italics omitted).

As the unpublished introduction to *The Sound and the Fury* makes clear, this thematic and stylistic breakthrough first presented itself to Faulkner as a form of imaginative empowerment. In the figural terms I am pursuing here, the "ecstasy" Faulkner experienced while writing *The Sound and the Fury* can be thought of as the discovery of a seemingly timeless aesthetic space from which to depict the disappearance of the pre-modern South—from which, as it were, to preside over the dismantlement of the great house. But as his career advanced, Faulkner found himself facing with increasing urgency the question of how an art founded on the disappearance of the world of his youth (and of his own youthfulness) could sustain itself. His difficulty in answering this question satisfactorily produces a bifurcation in settings in the second half of his career. On the one hand, it produces a search for a high place—the "pinnacle" of the Nobel Prize

Speech, the mountain of *A Fable*—from which to engage once again in comprehensive, authoritative, and time-defying acts of visionary seeing. On the other hand, it produces the prison setting, into which Faulkner repeatedly inserts mute relics of an earlier age, who either must learn to speak across a generational or ideological gap or who must resign themselves to bearing silent witness to the obliteration of the meaning they embody.[2]

By releasing Mink Snopes from prison, sending him back to Jefferson, and allowing him to confront Flem Snopes inside Flem's mansion, Faulkner engages in a revisionary journey back along the line of development I have just sketched. This journey bears a complex relation to Faulkner's artistic situation at the end of his career. In a letter written in the fall of 1961, approximately two months after he had finished *The Reivers,* Faulkner said, "I am not working on anything now, busy with horses, fox hunting. I wont work until I get hot on something. . . . I will wait until the stuff is ready, until I can follow instead of trying to drive it" (*Selected Letters* 458). The relaxed trust in his creativity expressed in this letter is one of the fruits of the process of working through Faulkner underwent in the late 1940s and early 1950s. During this period, Faulkner sought to defy the loss of self and subject matter he felt himself to be undergoing by engaging in acts of imaginative self-transcendence—most notably, by writing *A Fable*. In turning from this daunting labor to the more modest but more achievable task of making fiction out of his own earlier works of fiction, Faulkner discovered that he had been vouchsafed a renewal of his talent. As a result, he was able once again to trust his creativity. "[I] have not taken fire in the old way yet," he says in a letter written when he was beginning *The Town,* "but unless I am burned out, I will heat up soon and go right on with it" (*Selected Letters* 390).

However grateful Faulkner may have felt for this final efflorescence of his talent, he also knew full well its secondary, derivative, and self-limiting character. Hence the renewed sense of confidence expressed in his later letters seldom comes unaccompanied by a tone of wistfulness and regret. It is "the last flare, burning of [his] talent" that he is experiencing, "the last miniscule" that he is scraping "from the bottom of the F[aulkner] barrel" (*Selected Letters* 407, 433). By releasing Mink Snopes from prison after thirty-eight years—a period comprising, as Irving Howe says, "the bulk of Faulkner's manhood" (114)—Faulkner creates an apt metaphor for this mingled sense of renewal and impoverishment. The world Mink confronts after his thirty-eight year absence is as alien and incomprehensible to him as the postwar world seemed to Faulkner. But in his slow, difficult return to Yoknapatawpha County, Mink displays an ability, again like Faulkner, to turn aside from this world and to recover fragments at least of an earlier life and an earlier South.[3]

The mechanisms by which Faulkner conducts this elegiac journey of return are Mink's illiteracy and his resistance to religion. Because of Faulkner's apparent willingness during the editing of *The Mansion* to adjust the novel to conform to *The Town* and *The Hamlet,* commentators have tended to interpret the inconsistencies that remain as lapses of memory rather than as deliberate authorial choices. Faulkner's own final view, as expressed in the prefatory note to *The Mansion,* was that the "discrepancies and contradictions" were signs of his having "learned . . . more about the human heart and its dilemma than he knew thirty-four years ago" and of his knowing "the characters in this chronicle better than he did then" (n.p).[4] This is certainly true of Mink's illiteracy. In *The Hamlet,* Mink is consistently depicted as having the ability to read and write; at the moment of the murder of Jack Houston, for example, he contemplates attaching a placard to Houston's breast "with his name signed to it" (222). In *The Mansion,* by contrast, he is just as consistently depicted as illiterate. Despite his face-saving statement, "I can read reading, but I cant read writing good," the truth is that all writing (except numerals) lies "not one jot less forever beyond him than Arabic or Sanskrit" (50).

In releasing an illiterate Mink into the postwar world, Faulkner resurrects the image for resistance to modernity he had discovered in *Requiem for a Nun.* Mink is "The Jail" translated into human form and set in motion. Because he cannot read, he is largely immune to the fallen language of modernity with which the surface of the South has been overwritten; conversely, his illiteracy (together with his long absence) heightens his ability to detect and interpret the unfallen, hieroglyphic signs hidden beneath this fallen language. Faulkner enacts this process of resistance and recovery in the manner of the journey itself. As in the case of the "dusty widening" at the center of Jefferson in *Requiem for a Nun,* the roads Mink travels are texts, on which (or by means of which) is written the history of the transformation of the South. The macadam and concrete roads of the modern age are "smooth and hard as a floor," causing Mink's "bones and muscles [to ache] all the way up to his skull" (104, 262), but the dirt sideroads leading away from the paved highway are "familiar out of his long-ago tenant-farmer freedom" (398). They are not covered with the "vehicles . . . of the rich and hurried" but are instead "marked with many wheels and traced with cotton wisps" (263, 398). Mink repeatedly turns out of the highway into these sideroads, as if thereby to reenter his own past. And he finally abandons the highway entirely, finding in a half-abandoned railroad track not only a practical means of entering Jefferson undetected but a route back into his youth. As he stands looking at the track, he remembers the occasion thirty-eight years before (its cause now ironically forgotten) when he spent a night watching trains enter and leave the Jefferson depot; and he sees in the track an image of his own life, "the two of them mutual, in a way even interdependent" (405).

Similar considerations apply to Mink's resistance to religion. Other than the tactical problems of buying a gun and of entering Jefferson undetected, the only significant impediment to committing revenge that Mink faces in the course of his journey is his encounter with the Reverend J. C. Goodyhay. In this encounter, Faulkner revisits the struggle over the question of belief that is a central subject of *A Fable* and *Requiem for a Nun.* Goodyhay and his flock are a home-grown, Populist version of the desire for social and political reform endemic in America in the postwar era. In their willingness to use a black schoolroom as a meeting hall and to include a black woman among their numbers, Goodyhay's followers reflect the agitation for racial reform that resulted from the revelation of the genocidal horrors perpetrated by the Nazi regime. More broadly, they reflect a left-oriented postwar challenge to prevailing social and economic values; as one of their members says, they consist of "a passel of mostly non-taxpaying folks that like as not would have voted for Norman Thomas even ahead of Roosevelt, let alone Truman, trying to bring Jesus Christ back alive in 1946" (272).

In his career as public spokesman on ethical and moral issues, Faulkner often expressed support for the spirit of reform Goodyhay and his congregation represent. But in Mink's resistance to Goodyhay's sermon, Faulkner expresses his hard-won awareness that his art could not serve ethics and morality by so direct a route. Throughout the novel, Mink's pride is that "he would not be, would never be, reconciled" (18). His resistance is economic and religious in character; it consists of his refusal to accept the system of peonage governing his relations with Jack Houston and to believe in God (or, in his suggestive phrasing, "Old Moster"). By bringing this intransigence into confrontation with Goodyhay's sermon, Faulkner creates a brief allegory of his own recent artistic history. In *A Fable, Requiem for a Nun,* and intermittently in his other postwar novels, Faulkner had struggled with the question of whether he should use his art to explore, and possibly to affirm, religious and political beliefs. Goodyhay's sermon recapitulates one pole of this struggle. The Christ of the sermon resembles the Corporal of *A Fable,* even to the extent of knowing the slang of World War I rather than that of World War II; and the lesson he teaches Goodyhay about the indomitability of the will resembles, in essence if not in detail, the lesson the Battalion Runner learns from the Corporal.

But Mink merely watches Goodyhay, "himself alien, not only unreconciled but irreconcilable" (281). Earlier in the novel, when his life is being threatened by Jack Stillwell, Mink gives the Warden an account of his religious history that includes the statements, "I taken it back. . . . I taken it back from God" (99). We should not allow Mink's homely idiom to obscure the fact that his statement echoes one of the most famous acts of repudiation in modern literature—the moment in Thomas Mann's *Doctor Faustus* when Adrian Leverkühn says of Beethoven's Ninth Symphony, "It will be taken back. I will take it back" (478). What Leverkühn "takes back" is of course not just the Ninth Symphony but the whole legacy of romantic optimism the symphony symbolizes, a legacy that World War II had seemed to undermine. Faulkner never engaged in so comprehensive a gesture of repudiation. Yet in depicting Mink's indifference to Goodyhay's sermon, he expresses his final view of the struggle over the question of belief he had undergone in the late 1940s and early 1950s. And he thereby reaffirms the tragic vision that informed his earlier fiction—a vision in which, as Gavin Stevens says near the end of *The Mansion,* "There aren't any morals. . . . People just do the best they can" (429).

Once Mink shows himself to be immune to the temptation embodied in Goodyhay's sermon, he is free to carry his journey forward to the double conclusion of his murder of Flem and of his departure for the West. Although the first half of this conclusion has a long history in Faulkner's fiction, reaching back to Thomas Sutpen's barred entry into the plantation house and beyond, it is not touched in *The Mansion* with any enlivening gesture of the imagination. But in the second half of this conclusion, Faulkner adds a last grace note to his use of Mink Snopes as an expressive instrument. After his encounter with Gavin Stevens and V. K. Ratliff, Mink begins to walk toward the West. Then "a little further along toward dawn" (434), he decides to lie down. As he prepares for a sleep that Faulkner intimates will be the occasion of his death, he adjusts his position to accord with his belief that "a man must face the east to lay down; walk west but when you lay down, face the exact east" (435).

Mink's decision to lie facing the "exact east" alludes to the folk belief that bodies should be buried with their feet pointing toward the East, so that at the Last Judgment they will rise facing Jerusalem and the Valley of Armageddon.[5] This intimation of an impending resurrection is consistent with the tone of Mink's final reverie, in which he imagines himself "mixed and jumbled up comfortable and easy . . . with . . . the beautiful, the splendid, the proud and the brave" (435), and it provides a fitting way for Faulkner to conclude both Mink's journey of revenge and his own elegaic journey back into Yoknapatawpha County. We will misread Mink's gesture, though, if we fail to bear in mind the secular and subversive character of Faulkner's understanding of himself as an artist. Here at the end of his career, Faulkner surely knows that such immortality as he can hope for will result not from religion but from art. It is not Jerusalem Mink turns toward, but Jefferson.

Notes

CHAPTER ONE. *The Power of Sound*

1. For a useful overview of Faulkner's aural imagery, see Slatoff 27–39. Other studies of sound and voice in Faulkner's fiction will be cited at appropriate points below.

2. The full history of romantic and postromantic adaptations of the idea of the muse remains to be written. In addition to his *Natural Supernaturalism,* Abrams's *The Mirror and the Lamp* is extremely useful. See also Barmeyer, Bowra, Graves, and the chapter entitled "The Muses" in Curtius. For a discussion of the secularization of literary images in the nineteenth and twentieth centuries, see Ziolkowski.

3. Blotner, "William Faulkner's Essay," 124. This fragmentary, incoherent, but revealing brief essay describes the transformation of *Flags in the Dust* into *Sartoris.* It also has been reprinted by Putzel, who differs from Blotner in a number of his readings of Faulkner's difficult script. All citations in this book are to Blotner's version.

4. William Faulkner, "An Introduction to *The Sound and the Fury,*" 412. Two versions of this extremely important document have been published, one in *Mississippi Quarterly,* the other in the *Southern Review.* The first of these is apparently a preliminary draft for the second; although less polished than the second version, it is in many ways more interesting and more revealing. Unless otherwise noted, all references in this book are to the *Mississippi Quarterly* version.

5. For further discussion of Faulkner's view of the imagination, see Chapter Four. Examples of Faulkner's fascination with the idea that the imagination might be able to transform external reality can be seen in *The Marble Faun* and in "Carcassonne," an early short story in which the only character, a nameless vagabond, imagines that his mind can slip free of his imprisoning body (*Collected Stories* 895–900). The most striking expression of the idea, and the one that most clearly displays the association Faulkner framed between it and images of sound, occurs in

Poem III of *A Green Bough.* As Cleanth Brooks observes, Poem III was occasioned by the entrapment and death, in January, 1925, of Floyd Collins, a cave guide in Kentucky (*William Faulkner: Toward Yoknapatawpha and Beyond* 28). Dominating the poem is a phantasmagorical vision of the entrapped man's imagination flaring forth to transform the cave in which he lies captive. At the beginning of the poem, "The cave [is] ribbed with dark," but almost at once it comes to be "ribbed with music" (16). When this happens, "The cave no more a cave is," for the "ribs of music / Arch and crack the walls" (16), freeing the mind of the prisoner to enter a world filled with harmonious sound. Here, "threads of sound . . . / Loop from the grassroots to the roots of trees"; "the song of birds / Spins silver threads to gleam from bough to bough"; and "drowning waves, airward rushing, . . . / . . . rake the stars and hear / A humming chord within the heavens bowled" (18). Caught in this self-created music, the prisoner scarcely seems to notice or to care when the sentinel at the mouth of the cave prepares to usher him forth into death.

6. The maternal overtones of the imagery in this scene suggest a link between Quentin's desire for union with nature and his sense of having been denied his mother's love. Faulkner creates an explicit link of this sort in *A Fable,* when General Gragnon associates the sound of a cicada with the maternal nurturing he was deprived of as an orphaned child. The cicada, Faulkner says, makes "a purring sound such as [General Gragnon] imagined might be made by the sleeping untoothed mouth itself around the sleeping nipple" (42–43). Faulkner's novels contain an unusually high number of scenes in which some form of threatening sound—often female in origin—descends from above on a defenseless child. In *Light in August,* for example, when the dietician hales Joe Christmas forth from the womblike enclosure of her closet, she hisses down at him in a "thin, furious voice" (114); in *The Unvanquished,* Bayard Sartoris says that his grandmother's angry voice "seemed to descend on [him and Ringo] like an enormous hand" (8). One wonders whether Faulkner's equivocal attitudes toward sound may not have originated in childhood experiences of maternal affection and discipline (cf. Martin's discussion of Faulkner's mother's influence on his development as an artist).

7. Simpson's essay appears in revised form in *The Brazen Face of History* (181–208). The quoted phrases are altered in the revised version.

8. For discussions of the inscription of nature inside culture in *Sanctuary* and *Light in August,* see Matthews, "The Elliptical Nature of *Sanctuary,*" and Duvall's two essays. My thoughts on this topic have been influenced by Miller's *Poets of Reality.*

9. The italics are Faulkner's. Unless otherwise noted, all italicized passages in quotations appear in the original text.

10. See Jane Millgate, "Quentin Compson as Poor Player," passim, and Bleikasten, *The Most Splendid Failure,* 95–96.

11. Blotner's biography exists in two forms: the two-volume edition of 1974 and the one-volume condensation (with new material added) of 1984. All citations in this book are to the two-volume edition.

12. I use the term "voice" in this chapter to refer both to the concept of narrative voice as traditionally defined and to Faulkner's sense of his artistic identity. In neither case do I intend the term to bear a literal signification. For an important theoretical discussion of the concept of fictional voice, see Genette, 212–262. For discussions of the role of voice in Faulkner's fiction, see four excellent essays by Ross: "The Evocation of Voice," "Oratory and the Dialogical," "Rev. Shegog's Powerful Voice," and "'Voice' in Narrative Texts." These studies will appear in revised form in a forthcoming book entitled *Fiction's Inexhaustible Voice;* I am indebted to Professor Ross for allowing me to read this book in manuscript. See also Ruppersburg, where voice is essentially equated with point of view. For discussions of the importance of *The Sound and the Fury* to Faulkner's development as an artist, see Bleikasten, *The Most Splendid Failure,* 142–143 and Martin, passim.

13. In the *Southern Review* version of the introduction, Faulkner describes writing as a repetition compulsion that is providing him with a diminishing sense of satisfaction. By the time he had written *Light in August,* he says, "I found that I didn't even want to see what kind of jacket Smith had put on it. I seemed to have a vision of it and the other ones subsequent to *The Sound and the Fury* ranked in order upon a shelf while I looked at the titled backs of them with a flagging attention which was almost distaste, and upon which each succeeding title registered less and less, until at last Attention seemed to say, Thank God I shall never need to open any one of them again" (710).

14. In "Faulkner and the Reproduction of History," John T. Matthews uses Walter Benjamin's "The Storyteller" and "The Work of Art in the Age of Mechanical Reproduction" to explore aspects of the topic I am discussing here. Matthews focuses his discussion on the role of the graphophone in *As I Lay Dying.*

15. For discussions of Faulkner's sense of creative decline, see Blotner, *Faulkner: A Biography,* 1117ff.; Minter, 192–251; and Wittenberg, 205–248.

16. For further discussion of *Requiem for a Nun,* see Chapter Four.

17. In an interview with Loïc Bouvard, a French graduate student, Faulkner cites Rimbaud as an example when saying that he may "end up in some kind of self-communion—a silence—faced with the certainty that I can no longer be understood" (*Lion in the Garden* 71).

18. For a representative sample of reactions to the silencing of the guns, see Moult, especially 37–39. See also Löhrke, 599–622 and 654–656. Moult's book was published by Jonathan Cape in 1923 and Löhrke's by Jonathan Cape and Harrison Smith in 1930. Faulkner was published by Cape and Smith from 1929 to 1931, so he may well have had an opportunity to read either or both of these books. Also, he was in Paris during November, 1925 and could have attended the impressive Armistice Day ceremony held that year at the Arc de Triomphe. For a description of the ceremony, which culminated in a minute and a half of silence, see "Armistice Day Abroad."

19. Faulkner's interest in the Spanish Civil War began early. In 1938, in his first public political gesture, Faulkner contributed a brief statement opposing Franco to a collection of letters about the war by American writers. A year later, in an extraordinary gesture, he gave the manuscript of *Absalom, Absalom!* to Vincent Sheean with the understanding that it would be sold to raise money for a relief fund for the Spanish Loyalists. See Blotner, *Faulkner: A Biography,* 1030 and Faulkner, *Essays,* 198.

20. The attempts by Mallison and his companions to recapture Linda for the world of myth gain in significance when viewed in relation to the history of the muse presented at the beginning of this chapter. In a large sense, Faulkner's transformations of the figure of the muse—from Caddy Compson to Laverne Shumann to Charlotte Rittenmeyer to Eula Varner Snopes to Linda Snopes Kohl—enact the quarrel with modernity I am exploring in this book. One thinks in this regard of Whitman's demand in "Song of the Exposition" that the "Muse migrate from Greece and Ionia" (173) and take up residence in modern technological America. "Bluff'd not a bit by drain-pipe, gasometers, artificial fertilizers," he says, "She's here, install'd amid the kitchen ware!" (174). Faulkner, it seems, could scarcely have agreed less.

21. For discussions of the theme of reading in Faulkner's fiction, see my "Reading in 'The Bear'" and David Krause's three studies of *Absalom, Absalom!* My argument differs from Krause's in emphasizing the way Faulkner's view of reading changed over time.

CHAPTER TWO. *The Root of All Evil*

1. For representative comments about Hollywood, see *Lion in the Garden,* 240–244 and *Selected Letters,* 165–166, 186–187, and 205.

2. In an early essay, Donald T. Torchiana examines the role of finance capitalism in *Pylon.* Although our readings differ considerably, I

am indebted to Torchiana's pioneering study for a number of insights. In "The Autograph of Violence," John T. Matthews examines the role of money in *Pylon* from a Bakhtinian perspective. I am indebted to Professor Matthews for allowing me to read this insightful study in manuscript. Other important studies of *Pylon* are the chapters by Cleanth Brooks (*William Faulkner: Toward Yokapatawpha and Beyond* 178–204, 395–405) and Ruppersburg (57–80) and the essays by Bleikasten ("*Pylon:* Ou L'Enfer des signes"), Gresset ("Théorème"), and Pitavy.

3. The other instances in the novel of descent from the sky also invoke this symbolism. The flour released by Jack Holmes during his parachute jump is described as "unrolling ribbonlike, light, lazy, against the sky" (39); Laverne is described as being "dragged along the ground" at the end of her jump and as lying "dressed from the waist down in dirt and parachute straps and stockings" (196).

4. *Pylon* is not a novel that provides very full psychological and social histories for its characters, but the few details we have about the reporter's past life suggest that his improvidence originates in a desire to remain dependent on his mother and to punish—in the surrogate figure of Hagood—the husbands who have come between them. See in this regard Hagood's odd, arresting account of the reporter's mother's visit to the newsroom (92–93).

5. For discussions of this background, see Blotner, *Faulkner: A Biography,* 865–877, and Cleanth Brooks, *William Faulkner: Toward Yoknapatawpha and Beyond,* 395–405.

6. For expressions of these attitudes, see the biographical sketches Faulkner submitted to the Four Seas Company in 1924 and to *Forum* magazine in 1930 (*Selected Letters* 7, 47); see also the *Bookman* version of his 1931 interview with Marshall J. Smith (*Lion in the Garden* 8–15).

7. The main property Faulkner worked on during his visit to Hollywood in the summer of 1934 was Blaise Cendrars's *Sutter's Gold,* an impressionistic account of the rise and fall of John Sutter. The book strongly emphasizes the destructive effect of the discovery of gold on Sutter's life.

8. Textbook definitions emphasize the centrality to philosophical materialism of the belief that everything is either matter or directly dependent on matter for its existence. See Edwards, *The Encyclopedia of Philosophy,* 5: 179–188.

9. In seeking to affirm the importance of the life of the flesh, Faulkner participates in a central development of modern culture, one commanding the attention of thinkers and artists as various as Marx, Darwin, Freud, Nietzsche, Rilke, D. H. Lawrence, and Henry Miller. For a good, broadly-based history of this development, see Kern.

My own thoughts on the matter have been influenced by Norman O. Brown's *Life Against Death,* Herbert Marcuse's *Eros and Civilization,* and Kenneth Burke's "The Thinking of the Body." I am also indebted to Thomas Frosch's book on William Blake for insight into the romantic origins of modern thought about the body.

10. The most striking association of money with excrement in *The Wild Palms* occurs when Harry Wilbourne finds the money he and Charlotte need if they are to run away together. After the abortive liaison in the New Orleans hotel room, Harry decides to dispose of the bricks he had used to weigh down his suitcase. The trash bin into which he puts the bricks is described as containing "the casual anonymous droppings of the anonymous who passed it during the [previous] twelve hours like the refuse of birds in flight" (50). When Harry drops the bricks into this "mass," it casts up with "magical abruptness" (51) the wallet containing $1278. In a baldly direct way, this scene reenacts the infantile view, elucidated by Freud in "Character and Anal Eroticism" and elsewhere, of evacuation as a precious activity, worthy of reward. For an acute, Marxist-oriented discussion of money and materiality in *The Wild Palms,* see Rhodes and Godden.

11. Faulkner's depiction of this contrast extends into almost every dimension of the novel's imagery and action. One thinks, for example, of the extended contrast in styles of housing, as between the "neat, tight, brown-stained wind-proof tongue-and-groove" construction (283) of the doctor's beach cottage and the ship-lap construction, open both metaphorically and literally to the wind, of the cottage Harry and Charlotte rent from him. Thomas L. McHaney uses the images of odor and decay associated with the scene of Harry and Charlotte's first meeting as a basis for suggesting that they are entering a wasteland world (*William Faulkner's "The Wild Palms"* 48). Yet Faulkner's lush organic imagery differs significantly from the imagery of aridity and sterility one associates with the Eliotic tradition. Similar considerations apply to Gail L. Mortimer's "Ironies of Transcendent Love." Mortimer provides much valuable commentary on the excremental imagery of *The Wild Palms;* but because she posits transcendent, ethereal love as an unchallengable good, she does not acknowledge the extent to which Faulkner depicts materiality positively. In both instances, the question of how we are to respond to the imagery associated with Harry and Charlotte involves the larger question of whether we should read the novel from inside or outside the modern tradition of the celebration of the body.

12. Flaubert's *The Temptation of Saint Antony,* a work Faulkner frequently cited as one of his favorites, ends with St. Antony relinquishing his dream of spiritual transcendence and voicing a desire "to be matter" (232). Faulkner alludes to this novel in the first scene in Wisconsin,

when McCord sarcastically urges Wilbourne to "eat through your hundred bucks and then move into the woods and eat ants and play Saint Anthony in a tree" (103). Henri Bergson, whose ideas about time Faulkner cited as influencing his own, may also have influenced Faulkner's views on the materiality of memory. In the suggestively-titled *Matter and Memory,* Bergson argues that "memory . . . is . . . the intersection of mind and matter" (xvi).

13. Faulkner's use of visceral imagery in "Old Man" supports the view I advance here. Throughout his journey, the tall convict is immersed in a world of physical sensation of the sort Harry Wilbourne must struggle to affirm. But in willingly returning to prison, he chooses, as David Minter says, "the smaller way of security and peace" rather than "the larger way of joy and pain" (172). The convict's fondling of a phallic substitute (the cigar given him by the Warden) and his scatological rejection of women ("Women ---t!" [339]) both measure the distance between his final outlook and Harry's.

14. For Freud's association of creativity with infantile narcissism, see *On Creativity and the Unconscious,* especially the essay entitled "The Relation of the Poet to Day-Dreaming" (called "Creative Writers and Day-dreaming" in the *Standard Edition.*) See also "Leonardo da Vinci and a Memory of His Childhood." For a helpful discussion of Faulkner's creativity in terms of object-relations theory, see Mortimer, *Faulkner's Rhetoric of Loss,* 1–11. Faulkner's most explicit association of creativity with anality occurs in "Afternoon of a Cow," a *jeu d'esprit* written a few months before *The Wild Palms* (*Uncollected Stories,* 424–434). Faulkner depicts himself in this story under two guises: as an earthy, id-oriented farmer and fantasist named "William Faulkner," and as a prudish, censorious amanuensis named "Ernest V. Trueblood." The central event of the story consists of a fear-stricken cow defecating on "William Faulkner"; we later learn that this event and the circumstances surrounding it will serve as the subject for the writing Trueblood will do the next day. For an intriguing, brief discussion of Faulkner's interest in anality, see Endel. For a considerably different interpretation of "Afternoon of a Cow" as a story about creativity, see Grimwood, *Heart in Conflict,* 3–17. This book contains a long, interesting chapter on *The Wild Palms;* Grimwood argues that the novel reveals a conflict between Faulkner's "pastoral" and "sociological" understandings of his southern subject matter (87–134).

15. Hartman's book is a study of the place of corporeality in the works of the four poets identified in its subtitle. The argument of the book has considerable relevance to this chapter.

16. In an interview given on November 17, 1937, when he was just beginning *The Wild Palms,* Faulkner is reported to have said that he

didn't "plan to return to [Hollywood]" and that he intended to remain "at his . . . Oxford home for some time, or until he completes his book at least" (*Lion in the Garden* 33–34).

17. Jacques Derrida's commentary on the association of writing with masturbation in Rousseau's *Confessions* is apposite here. For Rousseau, writing and masturbation are both substitutes for more authentic forms of experience—writing for speech, masturbation for "hetero-eroticism" (the term is Derrida's). Derrida deconstructs both aspects of this parallel, arguing in relation to writing and speech that "there has never been anything but writing" in the sense that "there have never been anything but supplements, substitutive significations which could only come forth in a chain of differential references" (159). As with writing and speech, so with masturbation and hetero-eroticism. Sexual intercourse cannot provide us with an experience of unmediated presence, "without symbol or suppletory," because "pure presence itself, if such a thing were possible, would only be another name for death. . . . Hetero-eroticism can be lived . . . only through the ability to reserve within itself its own supplementary protection" (155). But if this is so, then "between auto-eroticism and hetero-eroticism, there is not a frontier but an economic distribution" (155). If auto-eroticism and hetero-eroticism are both supplementary activities, then the one is not exclusively a substitute for the other. Each is an independent mode of sexual activity, with its own *raison d'etre*. Derrida's argument encourages me in my view that Harry's act of masturbation should not be understood simply as a memorialization of Charlotte Rittenmeyer (or of Meta Carpenter). Cf. John T. Irwin's discussion of the auto-erotic character of Faulkner's artistic self-understanding (*Doubling and Incest* 158–72). Cf. also Watson's discussion of the relation between auto-eroticism and writing in *Flags in the Dust* (*William Faulkner: Letters and Fictions* 69–75). For an application of the concept of supplementarity to several of Faulkner's novels (although not to *The Wild Palms*), see Matthews, *The Play of Faulkner's Language*.

18. For a fuller description of these circumstances, see Chapter Three.

CHAPTER THREE. *The Dream of Freedom*

1. The correspondence I describe here is based on the portrait of Roth Edmonds in "The Fire and the Hearth," not on the harsher one in "Delta Autumn." But even this latter figure at one time directly reflected Faulkner's experience. As Joanne V. Creighton observes, in an

early draft of "Delta Autumn" Faulkner described the Roth Edmonds character—then called Don Boyd—as having volunteered for service as an aviator in World War I (140). For discussions of the influence of Ned Barnett and Caroline Barr on the characterizations of Lucas and Molly Beauchamp, see Blotner, *Faulkner: A Biography,* 1034–1037 and 1091; Minter, 183–184; and Wittenberg, 193–194. See also Faulkner's "Mississippi" (*Essays* 11–43).

2. This account of Faulkner's situation in the early 1940s is based on Blotner, *Faulkner: A Biography,* 1028–1107.

3. For a fuller version of Cowley's view, see *The Faulkner-Cowley File,* 3–12.

4. The size of Faulkner's Oxford holdings may actually have been somewhat smaller. According to Blotner, on August 1, 1940, the *Oxford Eagle* reported the size of Rowan Oak as "nearly twenty-four acres" (*Faulkner: A Biography* 1058).

5. For Faulkner's guilt over his brother's death, see Blotner, *Faulkner: A Biography,* 916–917. How extensive his financial support for his sister-in-law and her child actually was, or how long he provided it, is unclear.

6. In a letter written around the summer of 1936, Faulkner told Meta Carpenter that his wife had purchased some modern furniture and a radio while he was in Hollywood. He then said, "I have given myself (I have a small soul after all) a certain amount of sadistic pleasure in ejecting from the house pneumatic divans and Cab Calloways and so forth" (Wilde and Borsten 103; see also Blotner, *Faulkner: A Biography* 1096, 1220).

7. Blotner observes this irony; see *Faulkner: A Biography,* 986. The quoted phrase is from *Requiem for a Nun,* 209.

8. For the suggestion that Faulkner started writing because it seemed to promise a carefree style of life, see his interviews with Cynthia Grenier and Jean Stein in *Lion in the Garden.*

9. Faulkner uses *style indirect libre* throughout "The Fire and the Hearth," aligning his third-person narrative with either Roth or Lucas as the situation requires.

10. Cf. Simpson, "The Loneliness of William Faulkner." I have always found valuable Simpson's observation that for Faulkner the "image of the artist is the image of the obdurate self" (136). This essay appears in revised form, with the quoted phrase altered, in *The Brazen Face of History* (209–231).

11. Although Faulkner had to have assigned Isaac McCaslin a role in *Go Down, Moses* before he wrote "The Fire and the Hearth," he in-

vented Lucas first. Ike does not appear in the short stories from which "The Fire and the Hearth" was derived, all of which were completed before Faulkner began work on the novel itself. See *Uncollected Stories,* 184–237 and 690–697.

12. See Blotner, *Faulkner: A Biography,* 1076–1095; *Uncollected Stories,* 690–697; and Creighton, 121–138. Creighton's analysis of the compositional history of *Go Down, Moses* is flawed by her reluctance to admit that the novelistic version of "The Bear" was written before the *Saturday Evening Post* version. For an exploration of the relation between Isaac McCaslin and Quentin Compson, see Hunt.

13. Much of the critical commentary on *Go Down, Moses* has been directed at exhibiting the moral and ethical deficiencies of Ike's act of relinquishment. In turning aside from this line of argument, I do not mean to imply that I believe Ike's (or Faulkner's) dream of an original, integral, blissful selfhood, anterior to social existence, to be an accurate description of reality. I believe it is not, in that I assume humans to be inherently social beings. But acknowledging the illusory status of the dream of original bliss does not lessen the significance of Ike's dilemma. Ike struggles with the question raised by Freud in "Civilization and its Discontents": how, other than by repression, can self and society be brought into a mutually beneficial alliance? My quarrel with much of the criticism of *Go Down, Moses* is that it has been rather too willing to accept repressive solutions to this dilemma. For a representative sample of ethical interpretations of the novel, see Cleanth Brooks, *William Faulkner: The Yoknapatawpha Country;* Sundquist; and Vickery.

14. A comparison with the novels of the late 1920s and 1930s can underscore this point. Faulkner's use of mythological and Biblical references in novels such as *Sanctuary* and *Light in August* constitutes an oblique rejoinder to T. S. Eliot's view, advanced in "'Ulysses,' Order, and Myth," that "the mythic method" is "a way of controlling, of ordering, of giving a shape and a significance to the immense panorama of futility and anarchy which is contemporary history" (177). In their cryptic, fragmentary, and self-canceling character, Faulkner's mythic and Biblical references provide no stable ground against which the actions of his novels can be understood. They serve instead to *increase* our sense of the disorderliness of contemporary history by conveying, as Calvin Bedient says of the "reflective rhetoric" of *As I Lay Dying,* "little more than a momentary and frustrated impulse to the 'universal'" (95). In basing the fiction he creates on the Biblical myth of the fall, Ike McCaslin attempts to rescind the skepticism of Faulkner's earlier novels and to reinscribe history inside mythology. This process continues in Faulkner's use of a Christian allegory in *A Fable* and, as I argued in Chapter One, in the mythologizing of Linda Snopes Kohl in *The Mansion.*

15. The imagery of "Delta Autumn" supports this reading. As the automobile he is riding in moves from concrete pavement to gravel road to mud-filled lane, Ike imagines that "the land had retreated not in minutes . . . but in years, decades, back toward what it had been when he first knew it" (341). The goal of this journey is a "∇-shaped section of earth" that seems to have "gathered and for the time arrested [what remains of the wilderness] in one tremendous density of brooding and inscrutable impenetrability at the ultimate funnelling tip" (343). Given the female characteristics Faulkner consistently attributes to the wilderness in *Go Down, Moses,* this delta can be seen to resemble a pubic triangle and Ike's entry into it a return to a womblike condition outside time. When Ike imagines that "the two spans" of his life and of the life of the wilderness are heading "not toward oblivion, nothingness" but toward "a dimension free of both time and space . . . where the wild strong immortal game ran forever" (354), he links his impending death back to the dream of an original bliss. "Grave-womb or womb-grave," says Harry Wilbourne in *The Wild Palms,* "it's all one" (138). I am indebted to Richard Godden's "Iconic Narrative" for calling my attention to the sexual meaning of the delta image. Professor Godden presented this paper at the International Faulkner Symposium held in Bonn, Germany in 1987. In discussion afterwards, Professor Thomas L. McHaney observed, in support of Professor Godden's reading, that Faulkner's triangular image inverts the shape of its ostensible source, the Mississippi delta, which widens as it moves southward.

CHAPTER FOUR. *The Uses of the Imagination*

1. *Faulkner's "Requiem for a Nun,"* passim. Although my reading of *Requiem for a Nun* is in some ways diametrically opposed to Polk's, I am indebted to him for his willingness to challenge the moralistic interpretations prevalent in the 1950s, 1960s, and 1970s.

2. The most important studies in English of *Requiem for a Nun* are the essay by Broughton; the chapter on the novel by Vickery; and the book by Polk cited above. See also the essays in French by André Bleikasten, Michel Gresset, Jacques Pothier, and Jean Rouberol in RANAM 13 (1980).

3. Faulkner was quite active as a writer between 1941 and 1948, working for Warner Brothers and beginning *A Fable.* But in my view the writing of *A Fable* was a source of blockage, not a solution for it. See footnote 13 below.

4. The contrast between Temple's and Gavin's views corresponds in a general way to the contrast between a romantic and an Aristotelian understanding of the function of the imagination. For a discussion of this contrast that was influential during Faulkner's formative years as an artist, see Babbitt.

5. For a useful discussion of the artistic theories expressed in *Mosquitoes,* see Irwin, *Doubling and Incest,* 160–169. The scene with the blonde-haired girl in the outhouse is a striking example of Faulkner's association of artistic creativity with anality.

6. For discussions of the challenge posed to modernism by World War II, see Kazin; Levin; and Quinones. Quinones argues that "the very negativity that marks so strongly the preliminary phase of modernism looks to future growth" (8). Modernism, he says, is a "break-up" that looks forward to a "break-through" (9). The disappointment of this expectation by the Great Depression and World War II forced modernist writers such as Faulkner to rethink—and tempted them to make more explicit—the ethical bases of their art.

7. My understanding of this interpretation of the fall (a commonplace of Blake criticism) derives largely from Bloom and Frye. The possibility that Blake influenced Faulkner has never been studied. This is surprising, given that the rediscovery of Blake occurred during the years when Faulkner was engaged in a strenuous poetic self-education, and given that Faulkner clearly was familiar with the other romantic poets. Faulkner owned two copies of the 1941 Modern Library edition of the poems of Donne and Blake; the second copy was part of a set of books, apparently personal favorites, that he acquired in 1959 for use during his stays in Charlottesville (Blotner, *William Faulkner's Library* 8).

8. For a representative expression of this view, see Michael Millgate, 222.

9. Stevens's reinterpretation of Temple's conversations merits comparison with Harry Wilbourne's final reverie and Ike McCaslin's rejection of his inheritance. In each instance, Faulkner situates an act of narcissistic self-absorption in a context that endows the act with positive ethical value. Stevens's replacement of Temple as speaker merits comparison with his similar replacement of Linda Snopes Kohl in *The Mansion.*

10. Not long after writing *Requiem for a Nun,* Faulkner underwent a few sessions of therapy, but he proved a recalcitrant patient, refusing to speak about his mother (Blotner, *Faulkner: A Biography* 1453–1455). Faulkner's simultaneous attraction to and repulsion against the idea that the imagination might serve therapeutic purposes extends back as far as the scene of the Reverend Shegog's sermon in *The Sound and the*

Fury. The idea receives its fullest expression prior to *Requiem for a Nun* in the final chapter of *Absalom, Absalom!*, when Quentin Compson lies in his dormitory-room bed, listening to the suggestively-named Shreve McCannon and brooding over the significance of his visit to Sutpen's Hundred. The question raised by this scene is whether Quentin is doomed to repeat the story he and Shreve have constructed or whether he can in some way work through its implications and thereby free himself of his imprisoning allegiance to the past. For further discussion of this point, see my "Contemporary History in *Absalom, Absalom!*" See also Strandberg, 71–76 and Wadlington, 170–219. Wadlington argues that *Absalom, Absalom!* invites the reader to "say No to catharsis after experiencing its temptation" (216).

11. The association of blackness and illiteracy with authenticity and pure being was common in the first half of the twentieth century. See, for example, Anderson and Percy. The American Negro, says Percy, has an "obliterating genius for living in the present. . . . He neither remembers nor plans. The white man does little else: to him the present is the one great unreality" (23; quoted in Kazin 65). For a discussion of the pernicious political implications of the myth of an innate link between blackness and illiteracy, see Gates. The issue of *Critical Inquiry* in which Gates's comments appear is subtitled "'Race,' Writing, and Difference"; it contains several articles pertinent to an understanding of Faulkner's use of racial motifs.

12. It should be emphasized that Faulkner presents Temple's view of blacks as a trope, not as an assertion about reality. In commenting in Japan about the "foolish, silly things" people believe about blacks, Faulkner said, "They would tell you that a different kind of blood runs in the Negro's veins from the white man's veins. Everybody knows that blood's blood. Any student of biology could tell them that" (*Lion in the Garden* 148). In *Requiem for a Nun* itself, Faulkner makes clear the metaphoric status of Temple's comments by following them with her retelling of the story of "Pantaloon in Black," in which Rider, a black, dies an anguished death in the Yoknapatawpha County jail because he "cant quit thinking" (199).

13. For representative expressions of these attitudes, see Faulkner's interviews with Loïc Bouvard and Jean Stein (*Lion in the Garden* 68–73 and 237–256). *A Fable*, the novel Faulkner labored on during much of his period of creative blockage, can be read as an outgrowth of his desire for imaginative self-transcendence. Like the Bible, the source of the novel's central allegory, *A Fable* aspires to be a book beyond books, a book with a meaning so universal and all-encompassing as to exist outside time. Faulkner said that his purpose in writing the book was "to shape into some form of art [my] summation and conception of the human heart and spirit" (*Selected Letters* 261). Speaking of the agonizingly

slow composition of the novel, he said, "I'm doing something different now, so different that I am writing and rewriting, weighing every word, which I never did before; I used to bang it on like an apprentice paper hanger and never look back" (188).

14. For a discussion of the centrality of the idea of defying death to Faulkner's understanding of his artistic vocation, see Hamblin. See also Wadlington, 13–25. The comment about Kilroy is taken from Faulkner's Acceptance Speech for the National Book Award for Fiction (*Essays* 143).

15. The disappearance of the traditional South under the onslaught of the postwar world is also a prominent theme in *Intruder in the Dust*. See Chapter Five.

16. For a discussion of the romantic and symbolist antecedents of the idea of an unmediated relation between the self and the world, see Hartman. For a discussion of the relation between this idea and inscribed language, see Irwin, *American Hieroglyphics,* and Donato.

17. The stranger's mythologizing of Cecilia Farmer relates directly to the struggle between Gavin Stevens and Temple Drake in the dramatic sections of the novel. By converting Cecilia from wife and mother into *la belle dame sans merci,* the stranger enacts in reverse the conversion Gavin Stevens tries to induce Temple to undergo. The theme of outlawry also forms a bridge between the prose and the dramatic sections. In both halves of the novel, the figure of the outlaw is associated with freedom—libidinal freedom in the dramatic sections, social freedom in the prose sections.

18. Barthes distinguishes between "writerly" and "readerly" ways of reading in *S/Z*. For an illuminating application of these ways of reading to Faulkner, see Krause, "Reading Bon's Letter."

19. Citations of *The Sound and the Fury* in this paragraph are to the 1967 Modern Library edition. The Vintage-Random House Corrected Edition does not contain the Compson Appendix.

CHAPTER FIVE. *The Scene of Instruction*

1. See Blotner, *Faulkner: A Biography,* passim; Wittenberg, 205–248; and Minter, 192–251. Most reminiscences of Faulkner written by members of his family stress his fondness for children and his patience in teaching them. See John Faulkner; Falkner; and Wells. Malcolm Franklin is conspicuous in his dissent.

2. The impulse to deconstruct parenthood is of course not limited to Faulkner. As Peter Brooks argues, an interrogation of parental authority—particularly the authority of the father—is a dominant theme of the postromantic novel. As he also notes, this theme is explicitly addressed in the library scene of *Ulysses* (a novel highly influential on *The Sound and the Fury*), when Stephen Daedalus meditates on the possibility that "paternity may be a legal fiction" (*Reading for the Plot* 62–89, 286–213; *Ulysses* 205).

3. The one exception to this observation is Quentin's rueful comment after his unsuccessful attempt to calculate how much weight he should carry in his pockets while drowning himself. This is, he says, "the only opportunity I seemed to have for the application of Harvard. Maybe by next year; thinking maybe it takes two years in school to learn to do that properly" (105).

4. Standing behind the scenes of instruction in *The Sound and the Fury* and *Light in August* is the assault on authoritarian theories of teaching launched in the first third of the twentieth century by John Dewey and other advocates of progressive education. As Dewey says, "the traditional scheme [of education] is, in essence, one of imposition from above and from outside. It imposes adult standards, subject matter and methods. . . . Learning here means acquisition of what already is incorporated in books and in the heads of the elders" (*Experience and Education* 4–5). But in the progressive model, he says, "to imposition from above is opposed expression and cultivation of individuality; to external discipline is opposed free activity; to learning from texts and teachers, learning through experience; . . . to static aims and materials is opposed acquaintance with a changing world" (5–6; see also *Democracy and Education* 69–99). Dewey's progressive model makes an oblique appearance in *The Sound and the Fury,* in the form of Caddy's patient and loving attempts to teach Benjy. (One recalls, for example, her explanation of cold: "She broke the top of the water and held a piece of it against my face. 'Ice. That means how cold it is'" [14].) But the single-mindedness of Faulkner's vision of education at this point in his career does not allow him to present Caddy's mode of instruction as a viable alternative to Mr. and Mrs. Compson's. It is simply another of the novel's many icons of loss, an echo of the sensuous, concrete, preliterate world from which Benjy and Quentin feel themselves to have been exiled.

5. As stated here, Faulkner's understanding of resistance to instruction resembles Otto Rank's theory of the birth trauma. One also senses an affinity between Faulkner's views and Freud's theory, as developed in "Beyond the Pleasure Principle" and "The Uncanny," of the death instinct. In his most general formulation, Freud says that the death instinct consists of "an urge inherent in organic life to restore

an earlier state of things"; in human beings, the instinct takes the form of the "Nirvana Principle"—i.e., "the dominating tendency of mental life . . . to remove internal tension due to stimuli"—and of the compulsion to repeat ("Beyond the Pleasure Principle" 36, 55–56; italics omitted). It should be noted that Freud did not accept Rank's theory ("Analysis Terminable and Interminable" 216). For an important discussion of the pedagogical implications of Freud's theories, see Felman—especially her comments on ignorance as consisting not merely of "a passive state of absence" but of "an active dynamic of negation, an active refusal of information" (29–30). See also the entries entitled "Compulsion to Repeat" and "Resistance" in Laplanche and Pontalis.

6. I wish to observe in passing the importance of *Absalom, Absalom!* to the development of Faulkner's ideas on education. In returning to the story of Quentin Compson, Faulkner calls into question the singlemindedness of his earlier depictions of the scene of instruction. Whereas in *The Sound and the Fury* we see only one Quentin (the vainly resisting one), in *Absalom, Absalom!* we see two: the one "who was still too young to deserve yet to be a ghost, but nevertheless having to be one for all that," and the one "preparing for Harvard in . . . the deep South dead since 1865" (9). Similarly, we see two ideas of education, not just one. The relation between Quentin and his father reenacts Faulkner's earlier view of education as an inscribing of parental identity on the mind of an unwilling child. (This view is most memorably presented in the scene in the Sutpen graveyard, when Mr. Compson teaches Quentin how to read the traces left behind by the dead.) But the relation between Quentin and Shreve in the second half of the novel (especially in the eighth chapter) enacts an alternative view of education, as a mutual, collaborative, exploratory exchange between equals.

7. The literature on the mid-life crisis and on generativity is vast. In addition to Erikson's *Childhood and Society,* I have found Jaques and Neugarten useful. In *Heart in Conflict,* Michael Grimwood says that *Go Down, Moses* "records a full-blown Eriksonian 'crisis of generativity'" (224).

8. Faulkner displays Mallison's discovery of the complicity of school in the established social order in a telling detail. On his way to the jail to meet his uncle and the sheriff, Mallison notices several of "the yellow buses supposed and intended to bring the county children in to school" (135). Only after a moment's reflection does he realize that the buses are in the square not because they have carried pupils to school but because their owner has used them to bring adults to town to watch the Gowrie family's expected revenge against Lucas Beauchamp.

9. For an opposed reading, see Cleanth Brooks, *William Faulkner: The Yoknapatawpha Country,* 279–294 and 420–424. Brooks views the

Yoknapatawpha County of *Intruder in the Dust* as "an organic society" (291) and does not question the authenticity of Mallison's reconciliation with it. My interest in the function of the South in Faulkner's fiction and in his artistic self-understanding arose in large part out of my dissatisfaction with the view Brooks advances in his criticism. I also have serious reservations about Walter Taylor's study of the role of the South in Faulkner's fiction. Taylor's book is an example, to borrow a phrase from Geoffrey Hartman, of "the adversary method applied to literary criticism" (quoted in McFarland, 254). It is ungenerous in its judgments and lacking in sympathy with its subject. For trenchant criticisms of Brooks's views, see Bleikasten, "For/Against"; McHaney, "Brooks on Faulkner"; and Duvall's two essays.

10. See Chapter Two, footnote 16. Derrida views the notion of an originary fullness as itself illusory, arguing that the apparent beginning and ending points of any chain of signification do not preexist the chain but are instead created by it. In his greatest fiction, Faulkner interrogates the idea of origin with similar rigor; but in the relaxed and elegaic atmosphere of the late novels, the notion of a lost state of bliss is allowed to stand essentially unchallenged.

11. The quoted lines appear in Poem XVIII of *A Shropshire Lad* (Housman 31).

12. Faulkner's equation of Jefferson with Snopes gains significance when viewed in relation to the history of Jefferson provided in *Requiem for a Nun.* As we saw in Chapter Four, this history has at its core an Abraham-like search for a saving remnant of "irreconcilables" sufficient to preserve Jefferson from assimilation by the modern world. The equation of Jefferson with Snopes implies the failure of this quest.

13. For discussions of the influence on *The Town* of Faulkner's relationship with Joan Williams, see Blotner, *Faulkner: A Biography,* 1612; Minter, 239; and Wittenberg, 229. See also Joan Williams's *roman à clef, The Wintering.*

14. The Oedipal model for the male scene of instruction has undergone significant challenge in recent years, most notably from people interested in the pedagogical implications of deconstructive theory (see Scholes and Ulmer). But for Faulkner the Oedipal model, although full of tragic implications, never relinquishes its dominance; the essence of teaching for Faulkner is always a linear transmission of knowledge and belief from one generation to the next.

15. Chick Mallison's description of the father as the son's "son-in-law" (rather than "son") offers a striking example of the acuity of Faulkner's thought on psychological matters. By imagining himself as his mother's father, the son achieves a more complete revenge against

his father than in Jones's patrilineal version of the reversal fantasy, for he makes himself the only blood male in the family. The son thus doubly dismisses his father, first by making his father posterior to himself in time and then by making his father an interloper in the family romance. Similar considerations apply in reverse to Faulkner's use of "daughter-in-law" instead of "daughter."

EPILOGUE. *The Poetics of Space*

1. See also Minter, 242–244. For a helpful discussion of *The Mansion* as an elegaic "meta-fiction," see Stonum, 185–194.

2. A symbolic moment of transfer between the plantation house and prison settings occurs at the end of *Absalom, Absalom!,* as Quentin Compson stares at the open window of his dormitory room while recalling his trip to Sutpen's Hundred. When the image of the window, with its promise of growth and change, merges with the image of Quentin's father's letter, with its counsel of cynicism and despair, the dormitory room converts from a space of potential liberation into a prison *manqué,* and the way is prepared for the full-scale entry of the prison setting into Faulkner's fiction in his next novel. For discussions of the role of setting in Faulkner's fiction, see James G. Watson's "Faulkner: The House of Fiction"; the chapter of Gail L. Mortimer's *Faulkner's Rhetoric of Loss* entitled "Identity and the Spatial Imagination"; and William T. Ruzicka's *Faulkner's Fictive Architecture.*

3. As Victor Brombert has shown, the motif of imprisonment figures prominently in romantic and postromantic literature, where artists use it to express their sense of existential or metaphysical confinement and their yearning for transcendence. Faulkner evokes a central document in this tradition at the moment of Mink's release, when Mink suddenly remembers "a tree, a single tree" (104), in which resided a squirrel he shot as a child. As Walter Brylowski observes, this tree resembles the "tree, of many, one" in Wordsworth's Intimations Ode (211). We may add that Parchman Prison (along with all of Faulkner's other jails and prisons) recalls the prison-house whose shades descend about Wordsworth's growing boy and obscure the visionary gleam.

4. For discussions of the editing of *The Mansion,* see Blotner, *Faulkner: A Biography,* 1721–1741 and Meriwether, passim. For Faulkner's comments on the editing process, see *Selected Letters,* 423–432.

5. I have known of this custom for years, but I cannot recall where I learned of it. Gittings mentions the custom in passing and cites Sir Thomas Browne as a source, but without identifying a text (139). I do not find the custom mentioned in Browne's "Hydriotaphia," although Browne does say that "Christians dispute how their bodies should lye in the grave" (294).

List of Works Cited

Abrams, Meyer. *The Mirror and the Lamp: Romantic Theory and the Critical Tradition.* New York: Oxford University Press, 1953.

———. *Natural Supernaturalism: Tradition and Revolution in Romantic Literature.* New York: W. W. Norton, 1971.

Anderson, Sherwood. *Dark Laughter.* New York: Boni & Liveright, 1925.

"Armistice Day Abroad." *Times* [London], 12 November 1925, 13.

Babbitt, Irving. *Rousseau and Romanticism.* Boston: Houghton Mifflin, 1919.

Barmeyer, Erike. *Die Musen: Ein Beitrag zur Inspirations theorie.* Munich: W. Fink, 1968.

Barthes, Roland. *S/Z.* Trans. Richard Miller. New York: Hill & Wang, 1974.

Bedient, Calvin. "Pride and Nakedness: *As I Lay Dying.*" *Modern Language Quarterly* 29 (1968): 61–76.

Bergson, Henri. *Matter and Memory.* Trans. Nancy Margaret Paul and W. Scott Palmer. London: George Allen & Unwin Ltd., 1911.

Bleikasten, André. "L'Education de Temple Drake," *RANAM* 13 (1980): 76–89.

———. "Fathers in Faulkner." In *The Fictional Father: Lacanian Readings of the Text.* Ed. Robert Con Davis. Amherst: University of Massachusetts Press, 1981, 115–146.

———. "For/Against an Ideological Reading of Faulkner's Novels." In *Faulkner & Idealism: Perspectives from Paris.* Ed. Michel Gresset and Patrick Samway, S. J. Proceedings of the First Annual International Faulkner Symposium. Jackson: University Press of Mississippi, 1983, 27–50.

———. *The Most Splendid Failure: Faulkner's "The Sound and the Fury."* Bloomington: Indiana University Press, 1976.

———. "*Pylon*: Ou L'Enfer des signes." *Études anglaises* 29 (1976): 437–447.

Bloom, Harold. *The Visionary Company: A Reading of English Romantic Poetry.* 1961; rpt. New York: Anchor-Doubleday, 1963.

Blotner, Joseph. *Faulkner: A Biography*. 2 vols. New York: Random House, 1974.

———. *Faulkner: A Biography* (One-Volume Edition). New York: Random House, 1984.

———. "William Faulkner's Essay on the Composition of *Sartoris*." *Yale University Library Gazette* 47 (1973): 121–124.

———. *William Faulkner's Library—A Catalogue*. Charlottesville: University Press of Virginia in cooperation with the Bibliographical Society of the University of Virginia, 1964.

Bowra, C. M. *Inspiration and Poetry*. London: Macmillan, 1955.

Brombert, Victor. *The Romantic Prison: The French Tradition*. Princeton: Princeton University Press, 1978.

Brooks, Cleanth. *William Faulkner: The Yoknapatawpha Country*. New Haven: Yale University Press, 1963.

———. *William Faulkner: Toward Yoknapatawpha and Beyond*. New Haven: Yale University Press, 1978.

Brooks, Peter. *Reading for the Plot: Design and Intention in Narrative*. New York: Knopf, 1984.

Broughton, Panthea Reid. "*Requiem for a Nun*: No Part in Rationality." *Southern Review* n.s. 8 (1972): 749–762.

Brown, Norman O. *Life Against Death: The Psychoanalytical Meaning of History*. 2nd ed. Middletown, Conn.: Wesleyan University Press, 1985.

Browne, Sir Thomas. "Hydriotaphia." In *Sir Thomas Browne: The Major Works*. Ed. with an introduction and notes C. A. Patrides. London: Penguin, 1977, 271–315.

Brylowski, Walter. *Faulkner's Olympian Laugh: Myth in the Novels*. Detroit: Wayne State University Press, 1968.

Burke, Kenneth. *A Grammar of Motives*. New York: Prentice-Hall, 1945.

———. "The Thinking of the Body: Comments on the Imagery of Catharsis in Literature." *Psychoanalytic Review* 50 (1963): 375–418.

Cather, Willa. *My Ántonia*. 1918; rpt. Boston: Houghton Mifflin, 1977.

Cendrars, Blaise. *Sutter's Gold*. Trans. Henry Logan Stuart. New York: Harper and Brothers, 1926.

Cowley, Malcolm. *The Faulkner-Cowley File: Letters and Memories, 1944–1962*. New York: The Viking Press, 1966.

Creighton, Joanne V. *William Faulkner's Craft of Revision*. Detroit: Wayne State University Press, 1972.

Curtius, Ernst. *European Literature and the Latin Middle Ages*. Trans. Willard R. Trask. Bollingen Series 36. New York: Pantheon Books, 1953.

Derrida, Jacques. *Of Grammatology*. Trans. Gayatri Chakravorty Spivak. Baltimore: The Johns Hopkins University Press, 1976.

Dewey, John. *Democracy and Education: An Introduction to the Philosophy of Education*. 1916; rpt. New York: The Free Press, 1966.

———. *Experience and Education*. New York: Macmillan, 1938.

Donato, Eugenio. "The Ruins of Memory: Archeological Fragments and Textual Artifacts." *MLN* 93 (1978): 575–596.

Duvall, John N. "Faulkner's Critics and Women: The Voice of the Community." In *Faulkner and Women*. Ed. Doreen Fowler and Ann J. Abadie. Proceedings of the Twelfth Annual Faulkner and Yoknapatawpha Conference. Jackson: University Press of Mississippi, 1986, 41–57.

———. "Murder and the Communities: Ideology In and Around *Light in August*." *Novel* 20 (1987): 101–112.

Edwards, Paul, Editor-in-chief. *The Encyclopedia of Philosophy*. 8 vols. New York: The Macmillan Company and The Free Press, 1967.

Eliot, T. S. "'Ulysses,' Order, and Myth." In *Selected Prose of T. S. Eliot*. Ed. with an introduction Frank Kermode. London: Faber and Faber, 1975, 175–178.

Endel, Peggy Goodman. "Review of *The Most Splendid Failure: Faulkner's 'The Sound and the Fury.'*" *Faulkner Studies* 1 (1980): 161–167.

Erikson, Erik H. *Childhood and Society*. 2nd ed. revised and enlarged. New York: W. W. Norton, 1963.

Falkner, Murry C. *The Falkners of Mississippi: A Memoir*. Baton Rouge: Louisiana State University Press, 1967.

Faulkner, John. *My Brother Bill: An Affectionate Reminiscence*. New York: Trident Press, 1963.

Faulkner, William. *Absalom, Absalom!* 1936; rpt. New York: Vintage-Random House, 1972.

———. *As I Lay Dying*. 1930; rpt. New York: Vintage-Random House, 1964.

———. *Collected Stories of William Faulkner*. New York: Random House, 1950.

———. *Essays, Speeches and Public Letters*. Ed. James B. Meriwether. New York: Random House, 1965.

———. *A Fable*. New York: Random House, 1954.

———. *Father Abraham*. Ed. James B. Meriwether. New York: Random House, 1983.

———. *Faulkner in the University: Class Conferences at the University of Virginia, 1957–1958*. Ed. Frederick L. Gwynn and Joseph Blotner. 1959; rpt. New York: Vintage-Random House, 1965.

———. *Flags in the Dust*. 1973; rpt. New York: Vintage-Random House, 1974.

———. *Go Down, Moses*. 1942; rpt. New York: Vintage-Random House, 1973.

———. *A Green Bough*. 1933; rpt. in *The Marble Faun and A Green Bough*. New York: Random House, 1965. Separately paginated.

———. *The Hamlet*. 1940; rpt. New York: Vintage-Random House, 1972.

———. "An Introduction for *The Sound and the Fury*." Ed. James B. Meriwether. *Southern Review* n.s. 8 (1972): 705–710.

———. "An Introduction to *The Sound and the Fury*." Ed. J. B. M. [James B. Meriwether]. *Mississippi Quarterly* 26 (1973): 410–415.

———. *Intruder in the Dust*. 1948; rpt. New York: Vintage-Random House, 1972.

———. *Light in August*. 1932; rpt. New York: Modern Library, 1967.

———. *Lion in the Garden: Interviews with William Faulkner*. Ed. James B. Meriwether and Michael Millgate. 1968; rpt. Lincoln: Bison-University of Nebraska Press, 1980.

———. *The Mansion*. 1959; rpt. New York: Vintage-Random House, 1973.

———. *The Marble Faun*. 1924; rpt. in *The Marble Faun and A Green Bough*. New York: Random House, 1965. Separately paginated.

———. *The Marionettes*. Introduction and textual apparatus Noel Polk. Charlottesville: Bibliographical Society of the University of Virginia and University Press of Virginia, 1977.

———. *Mosquitoes*. 1927; rpt. New York: Liveright, 1965.

———. "Nympholepsy." Ed. J. B. M. [James B. Meriwether]. *Mississippi Quarterly* 26 (1973): 403–409.

———. *The Portable Faulkner*. Ed. Malcolm Cowley. Revised and expanded ed. New York: The Viking Press, 1967.

———. *Pylon*. 1935; rpt. New York: Random House, 1965.

———. *The Reivers*. 1962; rpt. Vintage-Random House, 1966.

———. *Requiem for a Nun*. New York: Random House, 1951.

———. *Sanctuary*. 1931; rpt. New York: Vintage-Random House, 1967.

———. *Selected Letters*. Ed. Joseph Blotner. New York: Random House, 1977.

———. *Soldiers' Pay*. 1926; rpt. New York: Liveright, 1951.

———. *The Sound and the Fury*. 1929; rpt. New York: Modern Library, 1967.

———. *The Sound and the Fury: The Corrected Text*. Ed. Noel Polk. 1929/1984; rpt. New York: Vintage-Random House, 1987.

———. *The Town.* 1957; rpt. New York: Vintage-Random House, 1974.

———. *Uncollected Stories.* Ed. Joseph Blotner. New York: Random House, 1979.

———. *The Unvanquished.* 1938; rpt. New York: Vintage-Random House, 1966.

———. *The Wild Palms.* 1939; rpt. New York: Vintage-Random House, 1966.

Felman, Shoshana. "Psychoanalysis and Education: Teaching Terminable and Interminable." In *The Pedagogical Imperative: Teaching as a Literary Genre.* Ed. Barbara Johnson. *Yale French Studies* 63 (1982): 21–44.

Flaubert, Gustave. *The Temptation of Saint Antony.* Trans. with an introduction and notes Kitty Mrosovsky. London: Secker & Warburg, 1980.

Franklin, Malcolm. *Bitterweeds: Life with William Faulkner at Rowan Oak.* Irving, Texas: The Society for the Study of Traditional Culture, 1977.

Freud, Sigmund. "Analysis Terminable and Interminable." In *The Standard Edition of the Complete Psychological Works of Sigmund Freud.* Trans. James Strachey. 24 vols. London: The Hogarth Press, 1964. 23: 209–253.

———. "Beyond the Pleasure Principle." In *The Standard Edition of the Complete Psychological Works of Sigmund Freud.* Trans. James Strachey. 24 vols. London: The Hogarth Press, 1964. 18: 3–61.

———. "Character and Anal Eroticism." In *The Standard Edition of the Complete Psychological Works of Sigmund Freud.* Trans. James Strachey. 24 vols. London: The Hogarth Press, 1964. 9: 167–175.

———. "Civilization and its Discontents." In *The Standard Edition of the Complete Psychological Works of Sigmund Freud.* Trans. James Strachey. 24 vols. London: The Hogarth Press, 1964. 21: 57–146.

———. "Creative Writers and Daydreaming." In *The Standard Edition of the Complete Psychological Works of Sigmund Freud.* Trans. James Strachey. 24 vols. London: The Hogarth Press, 1964. 9: 141–153.

———. "Leonardo da Vinci and a Memory of His Childhood." In *The Standard Edition of the Complete Psychological Works of Sigmund Freud.* Trans. James Strachey. 24 vols. London: The Hogarth Press, 1964. 11: 59–137.

———. *On Creativity and the Unconscious: Papers on the Psychology of Art, Literature, Love, Religion.* Selected by Benjamin Nelson. New York: Harper & Row, 1958.

———. "The Uncanny." In *The Standard Edition of the Complete Psychological Works of Sigmund Freud.* Trans. James Strachey. 24 vols. London: The Hogarth Press, 1964. 17: 217–256.

Frosch, Thomas. *The Awakening of Albion: The Renovation of the Body in the Poetry of William Blake*. Ithaca: Cornell University Press, 1974.

Frye, Northrop. *Fearful Symmetry: A Study of William Blake*. 1947; rpt. Princeton: Princeton University Press, 1969.

Gates, Henry Louis, Jr. "Editor's Introduction: Writing 'Race' and the Difference It Makes." *Critical Inquiry* 12 (1985): 1–20 [Special issue on "'Race,' Writing, and Difference"].

Genette, Gérard. *Narrative Discourse: An Essay in Method*. Trans. Jane E. Lewin. Ithaca: Cornell University Press, 1980.

Gittings, Clare. *Death, Burial, and the Individual in Early Modern England*. London: Croom Helm, 1984.

Godden, Richard. "Iconic Narrative: Or How Faulkner Fought the Second Civil War." In *Faulkner's Discourse: International Perspectives*. Ed. Lothar Hönnighausen. Tübingen: Niemeyer, forthcoming.

Graves, Robert. *The White Goddess: A Historical Grammar of Poetic Myth*. Revised and enlarged ed. New York: Farrar, 1966.

Gresset, Michel. "Genèse et avatars de *Requiem for a Nun*." *RANAM* 13 (1980): 5–37.

———. "Théorème." *RANAM* 9 (1976): 73–94.

Grimwood, Michael. *Heart in Conflict: Faulkner's Struggles with Vocation*. Athens: The University of Georgia Press, 1987.

Hamblin, Robert W. "'Saying No to Death': Toward William Faulkner's Theory of Fiction." In *"A Cosmos of My Own": Faulkner and Yoknapatawpha, 1980*. Ed. Doreen Fowler and Ann J. Abadie. Proceedings of the Seventh Annual Faulkner and Yoknapatawpha Conference. Jackson: University Press of Mississippi, 1981, 3–35.

Harrington, Gary. "Distant Mirrors: The Intertextual Relationship of Quentin Compson and Harry Wilbourne." *The Faulkner Journal* 1, no. 1 (1985): 41–45.

Hartman, Geoffrey. *The Unmediated Vision: An Interpretation of Wordsworth, Hopkins, Rilke, and Valery*. New Haven: Yale University Press, 1954.

Hemingway, Ernest. *Selected Letters, 1917–61*. Ed. Carlos Baker. New York: Charles Scribner's Sons, 1981.

Housman, A. E. *Collected Poems*. New York: Holt, Rinehart and Winston, 1965.

Howe, Irving. *William Faulkner: A Critical Study*. 3rd ed. Chicago: University of Chicago Press, 1975.

Hunt, John W. "The Disappearance of Quentin Compson." In *Critical Essays on William Faulkner: The Compson Family*. Ed. Arthur F. Kinney. Boston: G. K. Hall & Co., 1982, 366–380.

Irwin, John T. *American Hieroglyphics: The Symbol of the Egyptian Hieroglyphics in the American Renaissance*. New Haven: Yale University Press, 1980.

———. *Doubling and Incest/Repetition and Revenge: A Speculative Reading of Faulkner*. Baltimore: The Johns Hopkins University Press, 1975.

Jaques, Elliott. "Death and the Mid-Life Crisis." *International Journal of Psychoanalysis* 46 (1965): 502–514.

Jewkes, W. T. "Counterpoint in Faulkner's *The Wild Palms*." *Wisconsin Studies in Contemporary Literature* 2 (1961): 39–53.

Joyce, James. *Ulysses*. New York: Random House, 1934.

Kazin, Alfred. *Bright Book of Life: American Novelists and Storytellers from Hemingway to Mailer*. Boston: Little, Brown, 1973.

Kern, Stephen. *Anatomy and Destiny: A Cultural History of the Human Body*. Indianapolis: The Bobbs-Merrill Company, 1975.

Krause, David. "Opening Pandora's Box: Re-Reading Compson's Letter and Faulkner's *Absalom, Absalom!*" *The Centennial Review* 30 (1986): 358–382.

———. "Reading Bon's Letter and Faulkner's *Absalom, Absalom!*" *PMLA* 99 (1984): 225–241.

———. "Reading Shreve's Letters and Faulkner's *Absalom, Absalom!*" *Studies in American Fiction* 11 (1983): 153–169.

Laing, R. D. "The Family and the 'Family.'" In *The Politics of the Family and Other Essays*. 1969; rpt. New York: Vintage-Random House, 1972.

Laplanche, J. and J. B. Pontalis. *The Language of Psycho-Analysis*. Trans. Donald Nicholson-Smith. New York: W. W. Norton, 1973.

Lawrence, D. H. *Pornography and Obscenity*. New York: Alfred A. Knopf, 1930.

Levin, Harry. "What Was Modernism?" In his *Refractions: Essays in Comparative Literature*. New York: Oxford University Press, 1966, 271–295.

Lilly, Paul R., Jr. "Caddy and Addie: Speakers of Faulkner's Impeccable Language." *Journal of Narrative Technique* 3 (1973): 170–182.

Löhrke, Eugene, ed. *Armageddon: The World War in Literature*. New York: Jonathan Cape and Harrison Smith, 1930.

McFarland, Thomas. "Coleridge's Plagiarisms Once More: A Review Essay." *The Yale Review* 63 (1974): 252–286.

McHaney, Thomas L. "Brooks on Faulkner: The End of the Long View." *Review* 1 (1979): 29–45.

———. *William Faulkner's "The Wild Palms": A Study*. Jackson: University Press of Mississippi, 1975.

Mann, Thomas. *Doctor Faustus*. Trans. H. T. Lowe-Porter. New York: Alfred A. Knopf, 1948.

Marcuse, Herbert. *Eros and Civilization: A Philosophcial Inquiry into Freud*. Boston: The Beacon Press, 1955.

Martin, Jay. "'The Whole Burden of Man's History of His Impossible Heart's Desire': The Early Life of William Faulkner." *American Literature* 53 (1982): 607–629.

Matthews, John T. "The Autograph of Violence in Faulkner's *Pylon*." In *Post-Stucturalism and Southern Literature*. Ed. Jefferson Humphries. Athens: The University of Georgia Press, forthcoming.

———. "The Elliptical Nature of *Sanctuary*." *Novel* 17 (1984): 246–265.

———. "Faulkner and the Reproduction of History." In *Faulkner and History*. Ed. Javier Coy and Michel Gresset. Proceedings of the Third International Faulkner Symposium. Salamanca: Ediciones Universidad de Salamanca, 1986.

———. *The Play of Faulkner's Language*. Ithaca: Cornell University Press, 1982.

Meriwether, James B. "Discussion Group I: Bibliographical and Textual Studies of Twentieth-Century Writers." In *Approaches to the Study of Twentieth-Century Literature*. Proceedings of the Conference on the Study of Twentieth-Century Literature. East Lansing: Michigan State University Press, 1961, 35–51.

Miller, J. Hillis. *Poets of Reality: Six Twentieth-Century Writers*. Cambridge: The Belknap Press of Harvard University Press, 1966.

Millgate, Jane. "Quentin Compson as Poor Player: Verbal and Social Cliches in *The Sound and the Fury*." *Revue des Langues Vivantes* 34 (1968): 40–49.

Millgate, Michael. *The Achievement of William Faulkner*. 1966; rpt. New York: Vintage-Random House, 1971.

Minter, David. *William Faulkner: His Life and Work*. Baltimore: Johns Hopkins University Press, 1980.

Monteiro, George. "'Between Grief and Nothing': Hemingway and Faulkner." *Hemingway Notes* 1 (1971): 13–15.

Mortimer, Gail L. *Faulkner's Rhetoric of Loss: A Study in Perception and Meaning*. Austin: University of Texas Press, 1983.

———. "Ironies of Transcendent Love in Faulkner's *The Wild Palms*." *The Faulkner Journal* 1, no. 2 (1986): 30–42.

Moult, Thomas, ed. *Cenotaph: A Book of Remembrance in Poetry and Prose for November the Eleventh*. London: Jonathan Cape, 1923.

Neugarten, Bernice, ed. *Middle Age and Aging*. Chicago: University of Chicago Press, 1968.

Percy, William Alexander. *Lanterns on the Levee: Recollections of a Planter's Son*. New York: Alfred A. Knopf, 1941.

Pitavy, François. "Le Reporter: Tentation et derision de l'ecriture." *RANAM* 9 (1976): 95–108.

Polk, Noel. *Faulkner's "Requiem for a Nun": A Critical Study*. Bloomington: Indiana University Press, 1981.

Pothier, Jacques. "Naissance d'un sujet collectif: Jefferson." *RANAM* 13 (1980): 48–63.

Putzel, Max. "Faulkner's Trial Preface to *Sartoris*: An Eclectic Text." *Papers of the Bibliographical Society of America* 74 (1980): 361–378.

Quinones, Ricardo J. *Mapping Literary Modernism: Time and Development*. Princeton: Princeton University Press, 1985.

Rank, Otto. *The Trauma of Birth*. 1929; rpt. New York: R. Brunner, 1952.

Rhodes, Pamela and Richard Godden. "*The Wild Palms*: Degraded Culture, Devalued Texts." In *Intertextuality in Faulkner*. Ed. Michel Gresset and Noel Polk. Proceedings of the Second International Faulkner Symposium. Jackson: University Press of Mississippi, 1985, 87–113.

Ross, Stephen M. "The Evocation of Voice in *Absalom, Absalom!*" *Essays in Literature* 8 (1981): 135–149.

———. "The 'Loud World' of Quentin Compson." *Studies in the Novel* 7 (1975): 245–257.

———. "Oratory and the Dialogical in *Absalom, Absalom!*" In *Intertextuality in Faulkner*. Eds. Michel Gresset and Noel Polk. Proceedings of the Second International Faulkner Symposium. Jackson: University Press of Mississippi, 1985, 73–86.

———. "Rev. Shegog's Powerful Voice." *The Faulkner Journal* 1, no. 1 (1985): 8–16.

———. "'Voice' in Narrative Texts: The Example of *As I Lay Dying*." *PMLA* 94 (1979): 300–310.

Rouberol, Jean. "Le Sud dans les prologues de *Requiem for a Nun*." *RANAM* 13 (1980): 38–47.

Ruppersburg, Hugh. *Voice and Eye in Faulkner's Fiction*. Athens: The University of Georgia Press, 1983.

Ruzicka, William T. *Faulkner's Fictive Architecture: The Meaning of Place in the Yoknapatawpha Novels*. Ann Arbor: UMI Research Press, 1987.

Sartre, Jean-Paul. "On *The Sound and the Fury*: Time in the Work of Faulkner." In *Faulkner: A Collection of Critical Essays*. Ed. Robert Penn Warren. Englewood Cliffs, New Jersey: Prentice-Hall, 1966, 87–93.

———. *Saint Genet, Actor and Martyr*. Trans. Bernard Frechtman. New York: G. Braziller, 1963.

Scholes, Robert E. *Textual Power: Literary Theory and the Teaching of English*. New Haven: Yale University Press, 1985.

Seymour-Smith, Martin. *Who's Who in Twentieth Century Literature*. New York: McGraw-Hill, 1976.

Simpson, Lewis P. *The Brazen Face of History: Studies in the Literary Consciousness in America*. Baton Rouge: Louisiana State University Press, 1980.

———. "Faulkner and the Legend of the Artist." In *Faulkner: Fifty Years after "The Marble Faun."* Ed. George H. Wolfe. University, Alabama: University of Alabama Press, 1976, 69–100.

———. "The Loneliness of William Faulkner." *Southern Literary Journal* 8, no. 2 (1975): 126–143.

Slatoff, Walter. *Quest for Failure: A Study of William Faulkner*. Ithaca: Cornell University Press, 1960.

Sontag, Susan. "The Aesthetics of Silence." In her *Styles of Radical Will*. New York: Farrar, 1969, 3–34.

Steiner, George. "In a Post-Culture." In his *Extraterritorial: Papers on Literature and the Language Revolution*. New York: Atheneum, 1976, 155–171.

———. "Silence and the Poet." In his *Language and Silence: Essays on Language, Literature, and the Inhuman*. New York: Atheneum, 1970, 36–54.

Stonum, Gary Lee. *Faulkner's Career: An Internal Literary History*. Ithaca: Cornell University Press, 1979.

Strandberg, Victor. *A Faulkner Overview: Six Perspectives*. Port Washington, New York: Kennikat Press, 1981.

Sundquist, Eric. *Faulkner: The House Divided*. Baltimore: Johns Hopkins University Press, 1983.

Tate, Allen. "The Profession of Letters in the South." In his *Essays of Four Decades*. Chicago: The Swallow Press, 1968, 517–534.

Taylor, Walter. *Faulkner's Search for a South*. Urbana: University of Illinois Press, 1983.

Tobin, Patricia. *Time and the Novel: The Genealogical Imperative*. Princeton: Princeton University Press, 1978.

Torchiana, Donald T. "Faulkner's *Pylon* and the Structure of Modernity." *Modern Fiction Studies* 3 (1957–58): 291–308.

Ulmer, Gregory L. *Applied Grammatology: Post(e)-Pedagogy from Jacques Derrida to Joseph Beuys*. Baltimore: Johns Hopkins University Press, 1985.

Vickery, Olga W. *The Novels of William Faulkner: A Critical Interpretation*. Baton Rouge: Louisiana State University Press, 1959.

Wadlington, Warwick. *Reading Faulknerian Tragedy*. Ithaca: Cornell University Press, 1987.

Watson, James G. "Faulkner: The House of Fiction." In *Fifty Years of Yoknapatawpha*. Ed. Doreen Fowler and Ann. J. Abadie. Proceedings of the Sixth Annual Faulkner and Yoknapatawpha Conference. Jackson: University Press of Mississippi, 1980, 134–158.

———. *William Faulkner: Letters and Fictions*. Austin: University of Texas Press, 1987.

Wells, Dean Faulkner. *The Ghosts of Rowan Oak: William Faulkner's Ghost Stories for Children*. Oxford, Mississippi: Yoknapatawpha Press, 1980.

Whitman, Walt. "Song of the Exposition." In *Leaves of Grass*. Ed. with an Introduction Gay Wilson Allen. New York: New American Library, 1958, 172–180.

Wilde, Meta Carpenter and Orin Borsten. *A Loving Gentleman: The Love Story of William Faulkner and Meta Carpenter*. New York: Simon and Schuster, 1976.

Williams, Joan. *The Wintering*. New York: Harcourt Brace Jovanovich, 1971.

Wittenberg, Judith Bryant. *Faulkner: The Transfiguration of Biography*. Lincoln: University of Nebraska Press, 1979.

Wordsworth, William. "Lines Composed a Few Miles Above Tintern Abbey"; "Ode: Intimations of Immortality from Recollections of Early Childhood"; "Selection from *The Recluse*" ("Home in Grasmere"). In *The Prelude, with a Selection from the Shorter Poems, the Sonnets, The Recluse, and The Excursion*. Ed. Carlos Baker. New York: Holt, 1954, 96–101; 152–158; 199–202.

Zender, Karl F. "Contemporary History in *Absalom, Absalom!*: Some Directions for Study." In *Faulkner's Discourse: International Perspectives*. Ed. Lothar Hönnighausen. Tübingen: Niemeyer, forthcoming.

———. "Reading in 'The Bear.'" *Faulkner Studies: An Annual of Research, Criticism, and Reviews* 1 (1980): 91–99.

Ziolkowski, Theodore. *Disenchanted Images: A Literary Iconology*. Princeton: Princeton University Press, 1977.

Index

Main discussions of Faulkner's novels are indicated by italic page numbers.